JN336512

Features and Roles of Filled Pauses in Speech Communication

Hituzi Linguistics in English

No. 1　Lexical Borrowing and its Impact on English　Makimi Kimura-Kano
No. 2　From a Subordinate Clause to an Independent Clause
　　　　　　　　　　　　　　　　　　　　　　　　　　Yuko Higashiizumi
No. 3　ModalP and Subjunctive Present　Tadao Nomura
No. 4　A Historical Study of Referent Honorifics in Japanese
　　　　　　　　　　　　　　　　　　　　　　　　　　Takashi Nagata
No. 5　Communicating Skills of Intention　Tsutomu Sakamoto
No. 6　A Pragmatic Approach to the Generation and Gender
　　　　Gap in Japanese Politeness Strategies　Toshihiko Suzuki
No. 7　Japanese Women's Listening Behavior in Face-to-face Conversation
　　　　　　　　　　　　　　　　　　　　　　　　　　Sachie Miyazaki
No. 8　An Enterprise in the Cognitive Science of Language
　　　　　　　　　　　　　　　　　　　　　　　　　　Tetsuya Sano et al.
No. 9　Syntactic Structure and Silence　Hisao Tokisaki
No. 10　The Development of the Nominal Plural Forms in Early Middle English
　　　　　　　　　　　　　　　　　　　　　　　　　　Ryuichi Hotta
No. 11　Chunking and Instruction　Takayuki Nakamori
No. 12　Detecting and Sharing Perspectives Using Causals in Japanese
　　　　　　　　　　　　　　　　　　　　　　　　　　Ryoko Uno
No. 13　Discourse Representation of Temporal Relations in the So-Called
　　　　Head-Internal Relatives　Kuniyoshi Ishikawa
No. 14　Features and Roles of Filled Pauses in Speech Communication
　　　　　　　　　　　　　　　　　　　　　　　　　　Michiko Watanabe
No. 15　Japanese Loanword Phonology　Masahiko Mutsukawa

Hituzi Linguistics in English No. 14

# Features and Roles of Filled Pauses in Speech Communication
A corpus-based study of spontaneous speech

Michiko Watanabe

Hituzi Syobo Publishing

Copyright © Michiko Watanabe 2009
First published 2009

Author: Michiko Watanabe

All rights reserved. Except for the quotation of short passages for the purposes of criticism and review, no part of this publication may be reproduced, stored in a retrieval system, or transmitted in any form or by any means, electronic, mechanical, photocopying, recording or otherwise, without the written prior permission of the publisher.
In case of photocopying and electronic copying and retrieval from network personally, permission will be given on receipts of payment and making inquiries. For details please contact us through e-mail. Our e-mail address is given below.

Book Design © Hirokazu Mukai (glyph)

Hituzi Syobo Publishing
Yamato bldg. 2F, 2-1-2 Sengoku Bunkyo-ku Tokyo, Japan
112-0011

phone +81-3-5319-4916  fax +81-3-5319-4917
e-mail: toiawase@hituzi.co.jp
http://www.hituzi.co.jp/
postal transfer 00120-8-142852

ISBN978-4-89476-407-1
Printed in Japan

# Contents

List of Tables                                                vii
List of Figures                                                ix
刊行に寄せて                                                   xiii
Foreword                                                       xv
はじめに                                                       xix
Acknowledgments                                               xxv

## Chapter 1   Introduction                                     1

## Chapter 2   Background                                       5
2.1. Chapter Overview                                           5
2.2. The Types of Disfluencies and the Terminology in Disfluency Studies  6
   2.2.1. Types of disfluencies                  6
   2.2.2. Terminology for disfluent regions      7
   2.2.3. Distinctive features of disfluencies   8
   2.2.4. Rates of disfluencies                 10
2.3. Features of Filled Pauses                                 11
   2.3.1. Rates of filled pauses                11
   2.3.2. Types of filled pauses                11
   2.3.3. Functions of different types of filled pauses  13
2.4. Speech Production and Disfluencies                        16
   2.4.1. Speech production models and disfluencies  16

|     |     |
| --- | --- |
| 2.4.2. Frequent locations of disfluencies | 20 |
| 2.5. Speech Perception and Disfluencies | 23 |
| 2.5.1. Effects of disfluencies on native listeners | 23 |
| 2.5.2. Effects of disfluencies on non-native listeners | 28 |
| 2.6. Chapter Summary | 30 |

## Chapter 3  Speaker Variation in the Use of Filled Pauses  33

|     |     |
| --- | --- |
| 3.1. Chapter Overview | 33 |
| 3.2. Introduction | 33 |
| 3.3. Method | 35 |
| 3.3.1. Material | 35 |
| 3.3.2. The definition and the classification of fillers | 37 |
| 3.3.3. Procedure | 38 |
| 3.4. Results | 38 |
| 3.4.1. General tendency | 38 |
| 3.4.2. Features of each type of fillers | 40 |
| 3.4.3. Results of correspondence analyses | 48 |
| 3.4.4. Clustering of presentations | 55 |
| 3.4.5. Features of each cluster | 58 |
| 3.5. Discussion | 61 |
| 3.6. Chapter Summary | 64 |

## Chapter 4  Speech Planning and Filled Pauses  65

|     |     |
| --- | --- |
| 4.1. Chapter Overview | 65 |
| 4.2. Testing the Boundary Hypothesis | 66 |
| 4.2.1. Adverbial clauses in Japanese | 66 |
| 4.2.2. Method | 68 |
| 4.2.3. Procedure | 69 |

| | |
|---|---|
| 4.2.4. Results | 70 |
| 4.2.5. Discussion | 71 |
| 4.2.6. Rate of clause boundaries with conjunctions | 73 |
| 4.2.7. Duration of silent pauses at clause boundaries | 75 |
| 4.2.8. Filler rate at discourse segment boundaries | 78 |
| 4.2.9. Features of syntactic and discourse boundaries in casual presentations | 82 |
| 4.3. Testing the Complexity Hypothesis | 86 |
| 4.3.1. Method | 87 |
| 4.3.2. Results | 87 |
| 4.3.3. Discussion | 93 |
| 4.3.4. Filler rate at bunsetu phrase boundaries | 94 |
| 4.4. Chapter Summary | 96 |

## Chapter 5    Effects of Filled Pauses on Listeners' Expectation about the Upcoming Speech    99

| | |
|---|---|
| 5.1. Chapter Overview | 99 |
| 5.2. Introduction | 100 |
| 5.3. Experiment 1 with Native Listeners | 102 |
| 5.3.1. Participants | 102 |
| 5.3.2. Design | 102 |
| 5.3.3. Auditory and visual stimuli | 105 |
| 5.3.4. Procedure | 107 |
| 5.3.5. Results | 110 |
| 5.3.6. Discussion | 111 |
| 5.4. Experiment 2 with Non-Native Listeners | 113 |
| 5.4.1. Participants | 113 |
| 5.4.2. Design | 114 |

|  |  |
|---|---|
| 5.4.3. Procedure | 114 |
| 5.4.4. Results | 115 |
| 5.4.5. Discussion | 118 |
| 5.5. Chapter Summary | 120 |

## Chapter 6  Conclusion  123

| 6.1. Summary | 123 |
|---|---|
| 6.2. Contributions | 125 |
| 6.3. Future Work | 127 |

| Bibliography | 129 |
|---|---|
| List of Relevant Publications | 137 |
| 参考文献 | 141 |
| 関連発表文献 | 143 |

# List of Tables

Table 2–1  Distinctive features of six subcategories of disfluencies in terms of the elements at the given region  9
Table 3–1  The classification of presentations and the number of samples  37
Table 3–2  The mean frequencies and the mean rates of seven categories of fillers  39
Table 3–3  Summary of the features of fillers  48
Table 3–4  The proportions of inertia of the first four dimensions for academic presentations  50
Table 3–5  The proportions of inertia of the first four dimensions for casual presentations  53
Table 3–6  The names of clusters and the numbers of their members in academic presentations  56
Table 3–7  The names of clusters and the numbers of their members in casual presentations  57
Table 4–1  Features of three clause types - whether the clauses can contain their own topics, subjects, and clauses. Plus indicates positive and minus indicates negative.  67
Table 4–2  Correspondence between clause boundaries based on traditional clause classification and the classification system of CSJ  69
Table 4–3  Classification of clause types employed in the present study  70
Table 4–4  Mean frequencies of four types of clauses  70
Table 4–5  Mean rates of three types of clause boundaries with conjunctions (%)  74

| | | |
|---|---|---|
| Table 4–6 | The mean number of each boundary type | 83 |
| Table 4–7 | The duration of filled pauses at four types of boundaries | 85 |
| Table 4–8 | Results of pair-wise comparisons by length group | 91 |
| Table 5–1 | Mean duration of speech stimuli in each condition and mean durations of filled pauses in simple and complex conditions | 109 |
| Table 5–2 | Correct response rate of Japanese participants in each condition | 110 |
| Table 5–3 | Correct response rate of Chinese participants in each condition (%) | 115 |
| Table 5–4 | Analysis of variance | 117 |

# List of Figures

Figure 2–1  Terminology for disfluent regions adopted from Shriberg (1994)     8
Figure 3–1  The rates of filler type groups in academic and casual presentations     39
Figure 3–2  The mean rate of fillers in total     40
Figure 3–3  The mean rate of *e*     41
Figure 3–4  The mean rate of *ano*     42
Figure 3–5  The mean rate of *ma*     43
Figure 3–6  The mean rate of vowel type fillers     44
Figure 3–7  The mean rate of *eto*     45
Figure 3–8  The mean rate of *sono*     46
Figure 3–9  The mean rate of prolongations     47
Figure 3–10  A symmetric map of the first and the second dimensions for filler types in academic presentations. The first dimension separates *e* from *ano*, *ma*, *eto*, *sono* and prolongations (indicated by dotted circles). The second dimension sets *eto* apart from *ano* (shown by solid circles).     50
Figure 3–11  A symmetric map of the first and the third dimensions for filler types in academic presentations. The third dimension separates vowel type fillers from the others.     52
Figure 3–12  A symmetric map of the first and the fourth dimensions for filler types in academic presentations. The fourth dimension sets *ma* apart from *ano*.     52
Figure 3–13  A symmetric map of the first and the second dimensions for

filler types in casual presentations. The first dimension separated *e* from prolongations and *ano* (indicated by dotted circles). The second dimension set *ma* and *sono* apart from the others (indicated by a solid circle). 53

Figure 3–14  A symmetric map of the first and the third dimensions for filler types in casual presentations. The third dimension separates *eto* from the others. 54

Figure 3–15  A symmetric map of the first and the fourth dimensions for filler types in casual presentations. The locations of *ano* and prolongations indicate their complementary distribution (indicated by circles). 54

Figure 3–16  The mean frequency of each type of fillers per 100 words in five clusters of academic presentations 56

Figure 3–17  The mean frequency of each type of fillers per 100 words in five clusters of casual presentations 57

Figure 3–18  The ratio of each cluster in the two presentation types 58

Figure 3–19  The ratio of male and female speakers in each cluster of academic presentations 59

Figure 3–20  The ratio of male and female speakers in each cluster of casual presentations 59

Figure 3–21  The ratio of three age groups (born in 1950s, 60s, and 70s) in each cluster of academic presentations 60

Figure 3–22  The ratio of three age groups (born in 1950s, 60s, and 70s) in each cluster of casual presentations 60

Figure 3–23  The ratio and features of clusters of academic (left) and casual (right) presentations 62

Figure 4–1  Mean rates of three types of clause boundaries with filled pauses (%) 72

Figure 4–2  Rate of boundaries with fillers in academic and casual presenta-

|   |   |   |
|---|---|---|
| | tions | 72 |
| Figure 4–3 | Rate of clause boundaries immediately followed by fillers or conjunctions | 75 |
| Figure 4–4 | Mean silent pause durations at three types of boundaries in fluent and disfluent conditions | 77 |
| Figure 4–5 | Rate of clause and discourse boundaries with fillers | 80 |
| Figure 4–6 | Filler rate at clause and discourse boundaries in academic and casual presentations | 80 |
| Figure 4–7 | The rate of boundaries with filled pauses (FP) and with conjunctions | 84 |
| Figure 4–8 | The duration of silent pauses with and without filled pauses followed at four types of boundaries | 85 |
| Figure 4–9 | The rate of three types of clause boundaries with fillers as a function of the number of words in the following clause | 89 |
| Figure 4–10 | Rate of clause boundaries with fillers before short (1–8 words), medium (9–16 words) and long (17– words) clauses | 90 |
| Figure 4–11 | Rate of clauses with fillers after 3 types of boundaries as a function of the number of words in the clause | 92 |
| Figure 4–12 | Rate of three types of clause boundaries with conjunctions as a function of the number of words in the following clause | 93 |
| Figure 4–13 | Rate of phrase boundaries with fillers as a function of number of bunsetu phrases between the modifier and the head | 95 |
| Figure 5–1 | An example of visual stimuli: The visual stimuli always consisted of a simple shape (round, square or triangular) and a compound shape (with two arrows attached to the simple shape). The two shapes were always displayed in the same colour. Kanj (Chinese) characters were allocated under the figures, indicating "left" for the left figure and "right" for the right figure. | 103 |
| Figure 5–2 | An example of editing of speech stimuli, with their transcrip- | |

tions, speech waves, and F0 contours. *sp* in the transcription stands for silent pause. The filler (original) version contained *eto* between "kiirokute" (yellow and) and "sankaku" (triangle). The pause version was created by substituting *eto* with silence of the same duration. The fluent version was produced by editing out *eto* with the adjacent pauses (a preceding pause in this sample) from the filler version. 108

Figure 5-3 Japanese participants' mean response times to simple and complex phrases from the onsets of the words describing shapes in the fluent, filler, and pause conditions. 111

Figure 5-4 Novice, intermediate, and expert Chinese groups' mean response times to simple and complex phrases from the onsets of the words describing shapes in the fluent, filler and pause conditions. 118

## 刊行に寄せて

人前で話すと緊張して，アーとかエーとか頻発しませんか？ このような，話の内容に直接かかわらない言い淀みをフィラーといいます。気づいていないかもしれませんが，友達と話したりする様なリラックスしたときでも，結構フィラーが入ります。質問にどう答えようかな，相手はどう思うかな，こんな言い方で理解できるかな，といろいろ考えて話すと思いますが，その間，黙っていると，相手は困ってしまいます。そこで，話の途中ですよというサインも兼ねて，アーとかエーとかいうのです。話の中で声が出ていない部分を pause といいますが，フィラーでは声が出ていますので，filled pause とも呼ばれます。話し方の癖で，フィラーを頻発する人がいます。あまり多いと，聞きにくいですね。工学者の間では，従来，フィラーは不要なものとして取り扱われ，音声合成にしても，フィラーを入れようなどということは考えられていませんでした。しかしながら，最近，ロボットなどが登場して，人間らしさを与えるにはフィラーが重要な役割を担っていることが段々分かってきました。それだけでなく，フィラーには，話の内容を把握しやすくするという役割もあると言われています。やたらフィラーが入るのはいけないが，適切なフィラーの挿入は必要ということです。ただ，フィラーは，話す人の文化，生活環境，癖など，色々な要因とかかわっており，千差万別です。適切なフィラーを入れればいいといってもどうすればいいか，工学者は困っていました。フィラーに関する研究は，特に日本語では本格的なものが全くありませんでした。本書は，これに対して明確な回答を与えてくれるものとなっています。まず，年齢や性別によってフィラーの使い方がどのように異なるかで，話者をいくつかのタイプに分類し，体系的な整理をしています。次に，句境界などの言語的な切れ目との関係を調べています。さらに，フィ

ラーが話の内容を理解する上で重要な役割を果たしていることを，ユニークな心理実験によって実証しています。これによって，音声対話の研究が進展することが期待されています。工学者の立場から書きましたが，フィラーは，人間のコミュニケーションの根幹にかかわるものですので，人文系研究者にとっても重要な研究課題だと思います。この分野で遅れていた日本語の研究が，本書によって，今後進展することが期待されます。文系，理系を問わず，ヒューマンコミュニケーションに関する研究をしている人の必読の書です。

東京大学
広瀬 啓吉

# Foreword

Spontaneous utterances are full of disfluencies. Speakers sometimes hesitate at the beginning or in the middle of an utterance, producing a pause or non-lexical items such as um and uh in English or stretching a sound. Also, they sometimes make mistakes in conceptualization, grammatical formulation, lexical choice, or articulation, which are spontaneously repaired or left uncorrected. All of these are characteristics of spoken language, which you hardly find in written texts such as newspaper articles, text books, magazines, technical papers, and so on.

As you may easily imagine, speech disfluencies have long been regarded as valueless or "peripheral" phenomena in language research. No textbook on linguistics has spent pages on these issues. Very few researchers, except for those who were interested in disfluency as a sort of speech disorder, have seriously considered them as a meaningful topic in linguistics or other related fields.

Paying attention to such peripheral phenomena, this outstanding research book by Michiko Watanabe opens up new directions in linguistics, psycholinguistics, and language education. In particular, she focuses on filled pauses in Japanese, such as anno and eeto, and tries to elucidate their functions in speech communication. Her positive stance to the value of speech disfluencies sharply contrasts with their low status in traditional linguistics.

Following an extensive survey on previous studies, Michiko starts with a sociolinguistic investigation of Japanese fillers. She examines 240 speeches from *The Corpus of Spontaneous Japanese* (CSJ), which is the first large-scale database to provide rich and fine-grained annotation of phonological, morphological, syntactic, and discourse aspects of spoken Japanese, comparing the frequencies of several types of fillers across three sociolinguistic variables, i.e., formality, gender, and generation. She also applies a novel methodology, making appropriate use of statistical techniques, in order to classify individuals according to their usage of different types of filled pauses. These analyses clarify how speakers' choice of filler types is largely affected by sociolinguistic factors. This unparalleled work will shed new light on disfluency studies, in particular, those based on statistical analysis of spoken language corpora.

Michiko then moves to another corpus-based study, in which she examines the rate of filled pauses at a clause initial position in relation to the type of the preceding clause and to the length of the clause to be construed. Following some influential works by predecessors, she presents two hypotheses concerning the cognitive process that underlies the production of these fillers: i) the boundary hypothesis and ii) the complexity hypothesis. The boundary hypothesis states that speech disfluencies are more frequent at deeper syntactic or discourse boundaries, whereas the complexity hypothesis expresses that the more complex the constituent, the higher the disfluency rate at the beginning. Precise statistical analyses using a large amount of data from CSJ reveal that these hypotheses are fully, or in part, supported, suggesting that speakers' production of fillers may be induced by severe cognitive load in speech planning. The work should have an enormous impact on psychological study of spoken language.

In the last part of the book, Michiko further considers the complexity hypothesis based on two psychological experiments. She assumes that if the association between speech disfluency and constituent complexity is recognized by listeners, they would predict a relatively long or complex expression in the presence of a disfluency. A carefully designed experiment involving 30 native speakers of Japanese shows that the listener's response to a complex expression is quicker when it is preceded by a filler than when it is not, supporting the hypothesis. An additional experiment that imposes the same experimental task on Chinese speakers who have been learning Japanese indicates that proficient non-native speakers can make use of cueing function of filled pauses as effectively as native speakers while less experienced non-native speakers cannot. These results suggest that listeners are, at some level of consciousness, aware of communicative function of disfluencies and that this skill depends on the proficiency of the language. The implications of this great work will reach not only to basic research in linguistics and psycholinguistics but also to applied research in language education.

The three studies presented in this book are one of the highest summits in the most advanced research on our everyday language. They are not just descriptive. They have linguistic and psychological theories behind. They also have significance in practical fields such as second-language education. There is no doubt that the author's great endeavor has established a firm position in those scientific disciplines for such peripheral phenomena as speech disfluency.

One more remarkable feature of this research to be emphasized at the end is its effective use of a large-scale database of spoken language. Obviously, it has become possible due to the appearance of *The Corpus of Spontaneous Japanese* (CSJ), incomparable speech database in its quantity and quality. In this respect, this book, in addition to its scientific importance, also provides excellent examples of how such a large-scale corpus can be most effectively utilized in empirical study of language. Particular attention should be paid upon its effectual use of rich linguistic annotations at various levels including morphology, syntax, and discourse. Sophisticated corpora like CSJ have made it handy to incorporate these more-than-superficial information into extensive and precise analysis of language, and the works demonstrated here in this book are definitely proven to be among the finest of such achievements. The readers of this book would certainly learn why the study of our everyday language should be based on empirical data and how those data go beyond our intuition about actual language use.

Absolutely, this is one of the most influential research books in language and communication.

Chiba University<br>
Yasuharu Den

# はじめに

　本書は，話し言葉に固有の特徴の一つである「言い淀み」について研究したものである。例を見てみよう。第1章でも紹介するが，次の一節は，大学の講義を録音した音声の一部を，できるだけ元の音声に忠実に書き起こしたものである。

<u>エート</u>，それでははじめます。<u>エート，ぜんかいー，エ，ア</u>，せんしゅうは，<u>アノ</u>，れんきゅうでおやすみだったんですけれども，<u>エ</u>，そのまえは<u>ですね</u>，<u>きゅ</u>，きゅうきょきゅうこうにしてしまってもうしわけありませんでした。

　上の一節中の下線部は，文の意味に関与しないため，通常の書き起しでは省略される部分である。このような要素が「言い淀み」と総称されている（小出，1983）。言い淀みは，話し言葉に頻出するにもかかわらず，音声コミュニケーションにおいて果たしている役割についての実証的研究は，特に日本語に関しては驚くほど少ない。その主な原因の一つとして，言い淀みの定量的分析を可能とするような大規模話し言葉コーパスがごく近年まで存在しなかったことが挙げられる。

　本研究では，2004年に一般公開された『日本語話し言葉コーパス（CSJ）』に収録されている講演音声データを対象に，まず，言い淀みの中でも最も頻度の高い，「エート」，「アノー」などのフィラーの分布の特徴を分析した。そして，高頻度で用いられるフィラーの種類には，場の改まり度や話者の性別・年齢といった社会言語学的要因が影響していることを示した。次に，句境界におけるフィラーの出現率を調べ，それが，統語的，意味的な境界の深さや後続句の長さと関連していることを明らかにした。この結果は，フィラーの

使用が後続発話生成の困難さの度合いに対応した事象であるという仮説を支持するものである。さらに，心理言語学的実験によって，聴き手にとっても，フィラーが後続発話の方向性を予測する上での手掛りとなっていることを示唆する結果を得た。

　6章からなる本書の構成および要旨は以下の通りである。

　第1章で，研究の動機，目的，対象を述べた。

　第2章では関連先行研究を概観した。まず，Section 2.2で，典型的な言い淀みの分類法と頻度についての研究を紹介した。つぎに，Section 2.3では，日本語のフィラーの種類と用法についての研究を概観した。Section 2.4では，発話生成モデルと言い淀みとの関連についての研究を紹介した。Section 2.5では，言い淀みが聴き手に及ぼす影響についての研究を，フィラーを中心に概観した。フィラーは，発話内容のプラニングが必要な談話境界や，文，節，句などの主要構成素境界に現れやすいこと，また，後続構成素が長く複雑なほど出現率が高いことがこれまでの研究で指摘されている。これらの研究より，フィラーの出現率に関し，「境界仮説」，「複雑さ仮説」の2つの仮説を提示した。境界仮説とは，「境界が深いほど，フィラーの出現率は高い」，複雑さ仮説とは，「後続構成素が長く複雑なほど，フィラーの出現率は高い」というものである。これらの仮説を第4章で検証した。

　言い淀みの種類や頻度には個人差の大きいことが指摘されている。第3章では，話者の性別・年齢や場の改まり度の違いと，高頻度フィラーとの間に何らかの対応があるかどうかを，CSJ中の講演の一部を対象に，分散分析とクラスタリングの手法によって調べた。よく用いられるフィラーには，場の改まり度の違いや話者の性別・年齢による偏りがあり，しかも，関連する要因はフィラーの種類によって異なっていた。話者のフィラー選択には社会言語学的要因が影響していることが示唆された。

　第4章では，境界仮説と複雑さ仮説を，節境界のフィラーの出現率を対象に検証した。境界仮説より，フィラーの出現率は，節境界＜文境界＜談話境界となることが予測される。節境界の深さに関しては，南 (1974) による，従

属節の主節からの独立度の概念を援用し，節境界を3つのタイプに分けた。すなわち，南では，従属節の主節からの独立度はA類＜B類＜C類とされている。したがって，従属節－主節間の境界も，この順序で深いことを想定した。ただし，A類は1講演あたりのサンプル数が少なかったため，分析対象から除外した。各タイプの境界におけるフィラーの出現率を調べた結果，B類＜C類・文＜談話境界となった。すなわち，全体としては境界仮説は支持されたが，C類の節境界と文境界とで，フィラーの出現率に有意差はなかった。文境界では節境界に比べ，ポーズが長く，接続詞の頻度も高い。文の切れ目では多少長い間をおいても不自然ではないため，話し手は，ポーズやそれに続く接続詞の時間を利用して後続発話のプラニングを行なっているものと考察した。

次に，節境界と文境界におけるフィラーの出現率と後続節長との対応を調べることによって，複雑さ仮説を検証した。B類，C類の節境界では，後続節中の語数が多いほどフィラーの出現率は高く，複雑さ仮説を支持する結果が得られた。しかし文境界では後続節長とフィラーの出現率との間に対応は見られなかった。フィラーの節頭・節中を合わせた出現率は，境界の種類を問わず，当該節長の増加に伴い単調に増加した。これらの結果から，言語レベルの発話生成単位は，節または節よりも小さいものであることが示唆された。

節境界，文境界のフィラーの出現率は，後続構成素長よりも境界の深さとの対応の方が大きかった。しかもその傾向は，境界が深いほど強かった。深い境界では，話者は次に何をどう話すかについて考えなければならないことが多い。言い換えると，概念レベルでのプラニングの付加が大きい。そのような箇所でのフィラーの出現率は，主として概念レベルのプラニング量に左右されるため，後続構成素長との対応は弱まることが推察された。

第5章では，聴き手による後続発話内容の予測にフィラーの存在が影響しているかどうかを調べた。フィラーに続く主要構成素は，フィラーがない場合に比べ，長く複雑な傾向にあった。フィラーの有無と後続構成素の複雑さ

とのそのような関係を聴き手が後続発話内容の予測に用いているかどうか
を，日本語母語話者と非母語話者（中国語話者）を対象に，聴取実験によって
調べた．実験では，コンピュータ画面に，単純な図形とそれらに2本の矢印
がついた，より複雑な形の図形がペアで提示された．続いて，「あのね，隣の
部屋から赤くて丸い紙持ってきてくれる？」のように，どちらかの形をした
紙をもってくるよう，話者が対話者に頼んでいる音声が提示された．被験者
は，言及されているのがどちらの図形かわかり次第，できるだけ早く，図形
に対応したボタンを押すよう教示された．刺激文には，図形を描写する語（上
の文では「丸い」）の直前に，フィラー「エート」がある文（フィラー条件），
フィラーと同じ長さのポーズがある文（ポーズ条件），フィラーもポーズもな
い文（流暢条件）の3条件が設定された．フィラーは長く複雑な構成素の前に
現れる傾向があるため，フィラーがあると，聴き手は複雑な図形の描写が続
くことを予測すると想定した．したがって，実際に複雑な図形の描写がフィ
ラーに続いた場合は，フィラーがない場合に比べて，図形を同定するのにか
かる時間が短くなると予測した．一方，フィラーに「丸い」のような単純な
図形の描写が続いた場合，フィラーと後続構成素との一般的な共起傾向とは
一致しないため，聴き手の予測ははずれ，反応時間の短縮はおきないと予測
した．ポーズ条件は，反応時間にフィラーの効果があった場合，その効果が
フィラーの持つ音声によるものか，時間によるものかを調べるために設定し
た．フィラーと同じ長さのポーズにフィラーと同様の効果があれば，フィラ
ーの効果はフィラーの持つ長さの効果ということになる．もし効果が異なれ
ば，その違いはフィラーの持つ音声によって生じるということになる．

　日本語母語話者を対象とした実験結果は，「フィラーがあると，聴き手は
長く複雑な句が続くことを予測する」という仮説を支持するものであった．
予測どおり，フィラーが複雑な句の前にある場合は，ない場合に比べ，反応
時間が有意に短かった．一方，フィラーが単純な句の前にある場合，反応時
間の短縮はおきなかった．どの条件においても，フィラーがある場合と，同
じ長さのポーズがある場合とで，反応時間に有意差はなかった．この結果か

ら，フィラーの効果は，主に，フィラーが発せられる間に流れる時間によるものであることが示唆された。一方，非母語話者（中国語話者）を対象とした同じ実験では，被験者の滞日期間の違いにより，異なる結果が得られた。滞日期間の長い上級話者の反応パターンは日本語母語話者のものと同じであった。これとは対照的に，滞日期間が短く，日本語の話し言葉にまだ慣れていない被験者グループの反応時間には，フィラーの効果も，ポーズの効果も見出されなかった。滞日期間が両者の中間である被験者グループでは，複雑な句の前にフィラーがある場合は，ない場合に比べ反応時間が短縮したが，ポーズにはそのような効果は観察されなかった。一方，単純な句の前にフィラーがある場合は，ない場合に比べ反応時間が長くなった。この結果は，フィラーがあったために複雑な句を予測していたが，予測がはずれたために反応が遅れたと解釈することができる。これらの結果から，中国人日本語話者も，日本語の話し言葉に慣れるにつれ，日本語母語話者同様，フィラーを後続句の内容予測に用いるようになることが示唆された。

　第6章では，本研究を要約し，その意義を述べ，今後の課題に言及した。本研究では，まず，場の改まり度や話者特性の違いによるフィラー使用の違いを浮き彫りにした。つぎに，発話生成理論を踏まえ，主要構成素境界のフィラーの出現率を定量的に分析することによって，フィラーの生起に影響する要因を明らかにした。最後に，フィラーが聴き手の先読みを助けるという仮説を，母語話者，非母語話者を対象とした聴取実験によって検証し，コミュニケーションにおけるフィラーのポジティブな働きを示唆した。聴き手に対するフィラーの働きについての研究は少なく，貴重である。とりわけ，非母語話者の聴き手に対する影響を調べた研究としては先駆的である。

　今後，研究をより包括的なものにするためには，まず，文節境界，語境界，語中のフィラーの分布と働きについて，さらに調べる必要がある。また，フィラー分布の分析を種類別に行なうことによって，各種フィラーの独自性が見出されることが期待できる。その際，音形の違いだけでなく，音響的特徴量に着目することによって，より幅広い視点からの分析が可能になると考え

られる。さらに，他の種類の言い淀み生起との関連を調べることによって，フィラーの働きがさらに明確になると考えられる。他言語の言い淀みとの対照研究は，外国語教育に役立つのはもちろんのこと，発話生成・理解プロセスの言語普遍性と個別性についての知見を深めるのにも有効である。また，独話だけでなく，対話における言い淀みの定量的研究が，コミュニケーションにおける言い淀みの働きの解明に不可欠なことは言うまでもない。

# Acknowledgments

I am sincerely grateful to the people who helped me completing this thesis.

Keikichi Hirose and Nobuaki Minematsu provided research facilities and environments even before I officially joined the laboratory as a member. Yasuharu Den offered a second academic home at Chiba University and has given a lot of useful advice concerning data analyses. He also let me join the CREST project, which enabled me to take part in many stimulating international conferences. Max Coltheart and Sallyanne Palethorpe provided precious advice with enthusiasm in research when I was planning the perceptual experiments. I thank Hisao Miyano for his helpful advice on statistics. I owe my programming skills to many of the laboratory members, especially to Shinya Kiriyama, Taro Mouri, Yuji Yagi, Shusaku Miwa and Takahiko Inagaki. Finally, my special thanks are given to Koji Watanabe, who continuously encouraged and supported me to continue the research.

I have studied as a post-graduate student at both the humanities department and the science department. I find it a great pity that there is huge difference between the two faculties in human resources and financial resources as well as education and research systems. I heartily hope that the research environments in humanities departments improve, lest many brilliant students should leave disappointed and discouraged without a degree.

This research was partly supported by JST/CREST, through the Expressive Speech Processing Project (2001–2005), the 21st Century COE (Center of Excellence) in Electrical Engineering and Electronics for the Active and Creative World, the University of Tokyo (2003–2007), and HAKUHO FOUNDATION (2007–2008). This book is published with support of Grant-in-Aid for Publication of Scientific Research Results by Japan Society for the Promotion of Science (2008, Grant No. 205048).

# Chapter 1

# Introduction

Spontaneous speech, unlike written sentences or speech read aloud from written texts, contains plentiful of redundant expressions such as filled pauses (fillers), repetitions, non-lexical prolongations and false starts. These phenomena are called disfluencies. We define disfluencies as expressions which can be deleted without changing the linguistic message of the utterance containing them. The excerpt below is from a university lecture. The lecturer is apologising for having cancelled the previous lecture. Its linguistic message is, "Now I'd like to start. Last week we didn't have a lecture because of holidays. And I'm sorry that I suddenly cancelled my lecture the week before last." What the lecturer actually said was as follows. Italics indicate disfluencies. The translation is given below.

*Eeto*, sore de wa hazime masu. *Eeto, zenkaii, e, a,* sensyuu wa, *ano,* renkyuu de oyasumi datta n desu keredo mo, *e,* sono mae wa *desu ne, kyu,* kyuukyo kyuukoo ni site simatte moosiwake ari mase n desi ta.

*Well*, now I'd like to start. *Um, last time, uh, oh,* last week, *uh,* we didn't have a lecture because of holidays, but *um,* the week before last, *you know,* I'm sorry that I *sud,* suddenly cancelled my lecture.

(A lecture given at the University of Tokyo in May, 1999, recorded and transcribed by the present author with permission of the lecturer)

As lectures are usually pre-planned and rehearsed, they are assumed to be less spontaneous than everyday conversation. However, they contain abundant features of spontaneity which can hardly be observed in speech read aloud from written texts.

Despite their abundance in everyday speech, disfluencies had long been ignored in linguistic research because they had not been regarded as parts of language (Takubo & Kinsui, 1997). Conversation analysts and discourse analysts, however, have been interested in the roles of disfluencies in speech communication (Brinton, 1996; Schiffrin, 1987; Stenstroem, 1994). Psycholinguists have been studying disfluencies since 1950's, regarding them as clues to emotional states of the speaker or mental processes of language production (e.g. Goldman-Eisler, 1968; Lounsbury, 1954; Levelt, 1989; Maclay & Osgood, 1959; Mahl, 1956). Some researchers in the field of foreign language education have recognised an abundance of disfluencies in everyday speech, because disfluencies sometimes cause difficulties for language learners in comprehending spontaneous speech (Brown, 1977; Buck, 2001; Rose, 1998; Voss, 1979).

In Japan, disfluencies have mainly been studied by speech engineers. As disfluencies are a source of recognition errors, they automatically need to be detected and deleted for effective speech recognition systems (Goto, Itou, & Hayamizu, 1999; Quimbo, Kawahara, & Doshita, 1998). It is only about the last ten or 15 years that papers on disfluencies in Japanese started to appear in the linguistic fields. However, they often lack empirical support to be persuasive because of paucity of samples. The recent release of *The Corpus of Spontaneous Japanese* (CSJ) (The National Institute for Japanese Language, 2004) has enabled researchers to conduct quantitative analyses of disfluencies, as it contains about 660 hours of spontaneous speech with its transcription and various linguistic annotations including disfluencies. This study takes advantage of this corpus.

The purpose of this thesis is to describe the features of filled pauses in Japanese and to find out their roles in speech communication. Filled pauses are chosen as a target because they are the most frequent type of disfluencies in Japanese (Maekawa, 2004).

The rest of the thesis is organised in the following way: Chapter 2 surveys the relevant research on production and perception of disfluencies, with particular attention paid to filled pauses. Chapter 3 investigates speaker variation in the use of filled pauses. Chapter 4 examines the rates of filled pauses at syntactic and discourse boundaries of different strengths to test two hypotheses concerning the production of filled pauses. Chapter 5 describes two perceptual experiments conducted with native and non-native participants to test the hypothesis that filled pauses contribute to listeners' prediction about the upcoming speech. Chapter 6 gives the conclusion of the research.

# Chapter 2

# Background

## 2.1. Chapter Overview

This chapter reviews studies on disfluencies relevant to the present thesis with particular attention paid to filled pauses. Section 2.2 outlines the types and features of disfluencies. Section 2.3 surveys studies on the features of filled pauses. This section is concerned with the study on the speaker and speech variation in the use of filled pauses discussed in Chapter 3. Section 2.4 reviews research on disfluencies in relation to speech production processes. This section has particular relevance to Chapter 4. Section 2.5 surveys studies on disfluencies from the points of perception and comprehension of speech. This section is related to the perceptual experiments reported in Chapter 5. Section 2.6 summarizes the chapter.

## 2.2. The Types of Disfluencies and the Terminology in Disfluency Studies

### 2.2.1. Types of disfluencies

There is a wide range of naming, scopes, and classification systems for disfluencies. The superordinate terms for "disfluencies" is varied, including "hesitations," "(self)-repairs," "(self)-corrections." Details of the terms and the usage in the English literature are found in Shriberg (1994). We use the term "disfluencies" as a cover term because it has been used in most systematic studies on disfluencies such as Fox Tree (1993), Lickley (1994) and Shriberg (1994).

The similar confusion in the terminology and the scope of disfluency studies are found in Japanese literature. Yamane (2002) grouped the terms which can be referred to "fillers" into eight categories as follows, according to the nature of the terms. Although Yamane listed them as terms for "fillers," a wider range of disfluencies seem to be included as well.

1) Traditional terms for "interjections," such as "kantousi" or "kandousi."
2) Expressions of hesitation such as "iiyodomi."
3) The use of assumed functions in speech such as "filling words" (batunagi go), "connecting words" (tunagi go), or "inserted words" (sounyuu go).
4) The use of "nonsense words," such as "idle words," (asobi kotoba) "noise words" (zatuon kotoba), "words without meaning" (mu imi go), and "redundant words" (zyoutyou go).
5) Expressions of the view that disfluencies are mere sounds, without any meaning, such as "interjected voice" (kantou sei).
6) An expression of the view that disfluencies are a type of pauses, "voiced pause." (yuusei kyuusi).
7) Expressions of the view that disfluencies are markers of discourse management such as "discourse markers" (danwa hyousiki).
8) The use of loanwords such as "hesitations" and "fillers."

No systematic research on disfluencies in Japanese had been conducted so far presumably because of lack of large spontaneous speech corpora. However, as mentioned earlier, the release of *The Corpus of Spontaneous Japanese* (CSJ) (The National Institute for Japanese Language, 2006) has made empirical studies on disfluencies in Japanese possible. Details of the corpus will be given in Chapter 3, in which the distribution of filled pauses in CSJ is analysed.

The following six subcategories of disfluencies are often listed in the relevant studies (e.g. Fox Tree, 1995; Lickley, 1994; Rose, 1998). Japanese samples from the excerpt of a lecture cited in Chapter 1 are categorised into four categories below. The other examples are from Utimoto et al. (2004). Italics are the samples in question.

1) Filled pauses (fillers): *eeto, e, ano* (um, uh)
2) Repetitions of a part of words, words, and phrases: *kyu*, kyuukyo (su*d*, suddenly)
3) Non-lexical prolongations: zenkai*i* (last t-i-*i*-*i*-me)
4) Deletions: *zenkaii*, e, a, sensyuu wa (*last time*, uh, oh, last week)
    Deletions at sentence initial positions are called "false starts" or "fresh starts."
5) Substitutions: Kare wa *Osaka*, Kobe no syussin da.
    (He is from *Osaka*, Kobe.)
6) Insertions: mikan o, iya *amai* mikan o (oranges, no, *sweet* oranges)

## 2.2.2. Terminology for disfluent regions

The three types of disfluent regions have been recognised in many studies across disciplines: the material that will be replaced, editing terms, and the replacing material (e.g. Levelt, 1983; Shriberg, 1994). Shriberg proposed a terminology and definitions of these regions, modifying those of Levelt, as shown in Figure 2–1. A Japanese sentence is given as an example.

"Reparandum" ("RM") refers to the entire stretch of speech to be deleted to arrive at the intended utterance. The "interruption point" ("IP") indicates the observable moment of interruption. "Interregnum" ("IM") refers to the region between the end of the reparandum and the onset of the repair with or without editing expressions. The "repair" ("RR") region consists of the stretch of speech which has syntactic and semantic correspondence to the material in the reparandum (Shriberg, 1994, pp. 7–9 and pp.59–60).

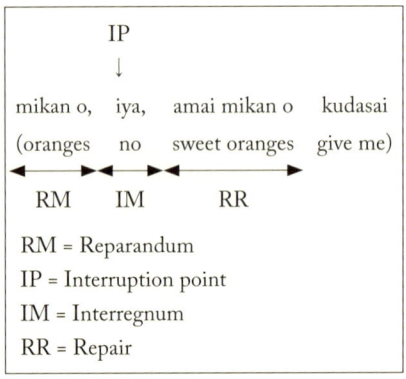

```
            IP
            ↓
mikan o,   iya,    amai mikan o   kudasai
(oranges   no      sweet oranges  give me)
◄─────►◄──►◄─────────►
  RM      IM        RR

RM = Reparandum
IP = Interruption point
IM = Interregnum
RR = Repair
```

Figure 2–1 Terminology for disfluent regions adopted from Shriberg (1994)


2.2.3. Distinctive features of disfluencies

In light of the definition and the terminology above, distinctive features of the subcategories described in Table 2–1 can be extracted. Fillers and prolongations can be regarded as phenomena only composed of interregna. Fillers and prolongations cannot be distinguished by this method. Deletions have elements of reparanda but no repairs. Repetitions, insertions and substitutions are all composed of reparanda and repairs. However, the difference lies in whether the reparandum and the repair contain the same linguistic elements: The reparandum and the repair are the same with repetitions, partly the same with insertions, and different in substitutions. These six subcategories can be grouped into two, depending on whether there is a change in semantic elements (meanings). Fillers, prolongations and repetitions do not involve semantic changes, whereas insertions, substitutions and deletions do, which may cause difference in the processing loads of listeners.

Table 2–1 Distinctive features of six subcategories of disfluencies in terms of the elements at the given region

Pluses (+) indicate the existence of the element; minuses (-) indicate the absence of the element. The rightmost column indicates whether the material in RM and RR are the same: Pluses indicate that they are the same, and minuses indicate that they are different.

| Subcategory | Reparandum (RM) | Interregnum (IM) | Repair (RR) | RM = RR |
|---|---|---|---|---|
| Filler | - | + | - | |
| Prolongation | - | + | - | |
| Repetition | + | | + | + |
| Insertion | + | | + | partly the same |
| Substitution | + | | + | - |
| Deletion | + | | - | |

It should be mentioned that quite a few studies include silent pauses in disfluencies (e.g. Goldman Eisler, 1968; Maclay & Osgood, 1954). However, a number of studies have reported that silent pauses indicate constituent boundaries, and that they are indispensable for listeners to comprehend the speech as well as for speakers to breathe in (e.g. Sugitou, 1990; 1994). Although some researchers proposed the distinction between "juncture-pauses" and "hesitation pauses" (e.g. Loundsbury, 1954), there is no objective way of distinguishing the two categories. Therefore, silent pauses are out of the focus of the present study, although some remarks will be made in relation to the roles of filled pauses.

### 2.2.4. Rates of disfluencies

It is reported that the mean disfluency rate in human-to-human telephone conversations in American English is about 5.5% (disfluencies are not counted as words). The difference whether the talks are task-oriented or free conversations hardly makes difference in the rates (Shriberg, 1994).

In simulated task-oriented telephone conversations in Japanese, about 50% of all the sentences contained redundant words (fillers) and about 10% of sentences included error corrections (Murakami & Sagayama, 1991). It should be noted that face to face conversations may reveal rates different from the figures above, because filled pauses are reported to increase when gestures are absent (Christenfeld, Schachter, & Bilous, 1991).

In the presentational speeches in *The Corpus of Spontaneous Japanese* (CSJ), the total rate of fillers and word fragments (results of repetitions, deletions, or substitutions) is 7.2% (Maekawa, 2004). Repetitions, deletions, and substitutions of words or phrases are not included in this figure. When they are included, the disfluency rate will be even higher. The speeches in CSJ have higher disfluency rates than those which have been found in studies with English data. However, to make a valid comparison, variables such as the speech genre (dialogues or monologues), the mode of communication (by telephone or face to face) and the degree of spontaneity should be controlled.

Regarding the gender of the speaker, it has been reported that men produced more disfluencies than women in British English (Lickley, 1994). In CSJ, the rate of fillers and word fragments are higher in male speakers' speech than in female speakers': 8.6% for male speakers, and 5.9% for female speakers (Maekawa, 2004). From the point of disfluency rate, female speakers are more fluent than male speakers both in English and Japanese.

## 2.3. Features of Filled Pauses

### 2.3.1. Rates of filled pauses

Among disfluencies, filled pauses have been reported to be the most frequent, repetitions the second and deletions the third in Switchboard (a corpus of human-to-human telephone conversations on various topics between strangers) and AMEX (a corpus of human-to-human air travel planning dialogues on the telephone) in American English. The mean filler rate of the two corpora is about 2.2%. The filler rate for Switchboard is about 1.6%, occupying roughly 40% of the total disfluencies. The filler rate for AMEX is about 2.8%, which composes of about 60% of the total disfluencies[1] (Shriberg, 1994).

In *The Corpus of Spontaneous Japanese* (CSJ), fillers consist of 6.3% and 5.9% of the total words (disfluencies inclusive) in academic and casual presentations, respectively (Maekawa, 2004). Academic presentations have a slightly higher filler rate than casual presentations.

In Japanese simulated dialogues, fillers are noted to occur in about 40 % of the sentences and that *e, eeto, ano, a,* and *ma* are the most frequent types (Murakami & Sagayama, 1991). Watanabe (1999) found that filled pauses occupied 8% of the time of the university lectures examined, and that lecturers used a filler every 3.8 second on average. In lectures, *ano, e, eeto, ma* and *sono* are the most frequent types. They account for roughly 90% of all the fillers (Watanabe & Ishii, 2000).

It has been reported that men use fillers at higher rates than women in American English conversations (Shriberg, 1994). In Japanese as well as in English, male speakers produce more fillers than female speakers: 7.2% for male speakers, and 5.0% for female speakers (Maekawa, 2004).

### 2.3.2. Types of filled pauses

The Japanese language seems to have a wider variety of filled pauses than English. The following sounds which have a gap filling function are regarded as "fillers" in CSJ:

a (:), i (:), u (:), e (:), o (:), n (:), to (:)*, ma (:)*,
u (:) n, a (:) (n) no (:)*, so (:) (n) no (:)*,
u(:) n (t) to (:)*, a (:) (t) to (:)*, e(:) (t) to (:)*, n (:) (t) to (:)*

Notes:
- All types of fillers above followed by *desune* (:) or *ssune* (:).
- Fillers with * above followed by *ne* (:) or *sa* (:) included.
- Sounds in parentheses are optional.
- ":" stands for a long vowel or nasal.

(Koiso et al., 2006)

We adopt this definition, and regard the sounds above as fillers. The following items, which were treated as fillers in some studies (e.g. Yamane, 2002), are not regarded as fillers in the present study.

- *de*, a contracted form of a conjunction *sorede* ("so" or "and")
- interjections such as *a* ("oh") and *iya* ("no")
- lexicalized items, such as *nan ka* ("somehow"), *tyotto* ("a bit"), and *nan te ii mashoo ka* ("what should I say")

Fillers are often preceded or followed by or sandwiched between silent pauses. We use the term "filled pauses" to refer to such sounds with adjoining silent pauses, if any. We use the term "fillers" to specifically refer to the sounds of "filled pauses."

Among the fillers listed above, a (:) (n) no (:), e (:), e (:) (t) to (:) and ma (:) have been reported to be the most frequent types both in dialogues and monologues (Murakami & Sagayama, 1991; Watanabe, 2001). In lectures and academic presentations, so (:) (n) no (:) is also listed as a frequent filler (Watanabe, 2001). The fillers listed above are transcribed as follows for simplicity hereafter in this study, disregarding the difference in durations of consonants or vowels in the original transcripts.

*a, i, u, e, o, n, to, ma,*

*un, ano, sono,*

*unto, ato, eto, nto*

*a, i, u, e, o* are the vowel sounds and *n* is one of the nasals of Japanese. *to* is a particle marking a quotation as well as a filler. *ma* has functions as an adverb meaning "fairly well" and an interjection for female speakers expressing surprise. *un* functions as an interjection meaning "yes," as well as a filler. *ano* and *sono* have functions as determiners similar to "that" and "the," respectively. *unto, ato, eto, nto* are assumed to be combinations of *un, a, e, n,* and *to*.

### 2.3.3. Functions of different types of filled pauses

Researchers have argued whether each type of fillers reflects different planning processes and consequently conveys different messages. In studies on Dutch monologues, Swerts (1998) found that *um* is more frequent after deep discourse boundaries than *uh*. It was also revealed that *um* is more typical for phrase initial positions than *uh*, whereas *uh* is more frequent at phrase internal positions. Shriberg (1994) reported that *um* is more typical for the sentence initial position than *uh*, although their positions largely overlap in American English. These studies revealed that *um* tends to appear at deeper discourse or syntactic boundaries than *uh*, and indicate that *um* may be used during the planning of larger units, whereas *uh* is more likely to reflect local lexical decision-making, as Shriberg (1994) inferred.

Clark and Fox Tree (2002) found that *um*s tend to precede longer silent pauses than *uh*s. They inferred that *um* signals longer delays while *uh* indicates shorter delays of upcoming speech.

In simulated Japanese dialogues, 60 % of *eto* occurred at the beginning of sentences. *ano* and *ma* were the most frequent at clause boundaries (40 % each). *ano* was also frequent after topic particles *wa* (15 %) (Nakagawa & Kobayashi, 1995). In university lectures, the rates of *eto* and *ma* were almost identical at sentence and clause boundaries (16–18%) (Watanabe & Ishii, 2000). These rates substantially differ from those of dialogues. In the lectures, the rate of *ano* at sentence initial positions was lower than the rates of *eto* or *ma* (8 %). *e* was the most frequent at clause boundaries (25 %) and the second most frequent at sentence boundaries (13 %). *sono* was hardly used at sentence initial positions. The results of the two studies indicate that *eto*, *ma* or *e* are more likely to be used before larger constituents such as sentences or clauses than *ano* or *sono*.

There is an argument that the functions of *eto* and *ano* are different, although they both signal that the speaker is searching for some knowledge or expressions in their mind, or doing calculation using the knowledge (Sadanobu & Takubo, 1995; Takubo & Kinsui, 1997). They claimed that *eto* is used to secure the working space in the speaker's mind, when the speaker is about to search for knowledge or start calculation with knowledge. On the other hand, *ano* is used when the speaker is searching for suitable expressions for the listener to convey the message. Their arguments were based on the observation that only *eto* is uttered when one is doing arithmetic calculation, or when one is on one's own. On the other hand, *ano* is typical when one speaks to someone or gives excuses. In terms of Levelt's (1989) language planning model, which will be discussed in the following section, these arguments can be put this way. *eto* is a filler while conceptualising, whereas *ano* is a filler for linguistic encoding. The distributions of *eto* and *ano* mentioned in the previous paragraph agree with their arguments. *eto* tends to occur at deeper syntactic boundaries at which speakers are more likely to be engaged in conceptualising a message, whereas *ano* are more frequent at shallower boundaries. However, their arguments need to provide criteria to distinguish the two stages of speech production and more empirical support.

The usage of the four common types, *ano, eto, e,* and *ma,* was described as the rule of thumb for Japanese learners and teachers as follows (Yokobayashi, 1994):

> *ano*: Used when speakers are retrieving suitable linguistic expressions. *ano* makes the utterance sound polite, when one asks questions or requests something. Not used when one thinks aloud on one's own.
> *eto*: Used when one thinks aloud. Not specifically polite to be used when one speaks to someone to ask questions or request something.
> *e*: Typical when one starts public speech. Less polite than *ano,* but more polite than *eto.*
> *ma*: Used when one mildly expresses one's evaluation or judgment.

Although such descriptions will serve for practical purposes for Japanese learners and teachers to a certain extent, they do not seem to be based on firm empirical research, and therefore, need examination. The descriptions above are also far from comprehensive as well. There is a study which states that when fillers in speech stimuli had been substituted by different types of fillers, no participants reported that the speech sounded unnatural (Ito, Minematsu & Nakagawa, 1995). This finding suggests that different types of fillers are interchangeable in many cases.

Although the results of the studies on Dutch, English, and Japanese fillers suggest that different types have different functions, in what aspect and to what extent their roles differ should be further investigated. In Chapter 3, it is examined whether sociolinguistic factors such as speech levels and speaker attributes have any relevance to the choice of certain filler types.

## 2.4. Speech Production and Disfluencies

This section surveys speech production models related to disfluency studies. This section has particular relevance to Chapter 4.

### 2.4.1. Speech production models and disfluencies

Disfluencies are prevalent in spontaneous speech, but rare in speech read from written texts. Because of this, they are believed to be applicable to on-line speech production. When speakers have some trouble in speech planning and need extra time, they are likely to be disfluent.

Three main stages are presumed in speech planning: 1) conceptualising a message, 2) formulating the appropriate linguistic expressions, and 3) articulating them (Garrett, 1982; Levelt, 1989). Disfluencies are claimed to occur at any of these stages (Clark & Fox Tree, 2002).

It is also postulated that the three stages can run in parallel for different components of speech generation. Each processing component is triggered into activity by a minimal amount of its characteristic input. In this view, speech production processes are "incremental" (Kempen & Hoenkamp, 1987).

There are a number of studies and proposals about speech production units (Levelt, 1989). Disfluencies, as well as speech errors, have been studied as indicators of such units. Generally, the points at which disfluencies are frequent are assumed as periods when major planning takes place. In the survey of speech production units, it seems important to be aware which unit of which stage the research focuses on. Some researchers assume an independent unit for each production stage, while others believe that the units are identical. The following part contains a survey of studies on speech production units relevant to this study.

Chafe (1980) did not assume plural units for speech production. Chafe observed that spontaneous speech is produced in a series of brief spurts, and called such spurts "idea units." This naming indicates Chafe's assumption that the units of conceptualisation, linguistic encoding, and articulation are identical. A single simple clause (one verb with accompanying noun phrases) or a part of a simple clause is postulated as a linguistic unit corresponding to the idea unit.

Levelt (1989) claimed that there is no single unit of speech production. Different processing components have their own characteristic processing units, and that these units may or may not be preserved at later stages. Levelt argued that phonological encoding may well undo grammatical units of the surface structure and impose an organization more appropriate for fluent articulation. However, the research on how the units at conceptualisation level relate to the units of grammatical encoding is not fully elaborated.

Ford and Holms (1978), Ford (1982), and Holms (1988) argued that basic clauses rather than surface clauses[2] correspond to the unit of conceptualisation. In the experiments, Ford and Holms (1978) had their participants press a response button as quickly as possible on hearing a "click" while telling a story. With less attention available for tone detection, reaction times were expected to be longer when speakers were engaged in conceptual planning. The reaction times were longer near the end of basic clauses than near the beginning of them. The reaction times at the beginning of surface clauses did not differ from those at the end of them. Based on these findings, they argued that basic clauses correspond to the unit of conceptualization. Following this study, Ford (1982) measured the rates of filled pauses at four types of boundaries: sentence, surface clause, basic clause, and within-clause. The filler rate was the highest at sentence boundaries. No significant difference was found between the rates at surface clause and basic clause boundaries. Ford also compared the rate of filled pauses before surface clauses consisting of one basic clause, with the rate before surface clauses containing more than one basic clauses. No significant difference was found between the two rates. Ford interpreted the results as an evidence that speakers do not plan more than one basic clause ahead, even if the surface clause contains more than one basic clause.

Smith and Wheeldon (1999) obtained results contradictory to those of Ford (1982). They had their subjects describe three moving objects and measured the sentence production latency. It took the subjects longer to start producing a sentence when the first noun phrase (NP1) contained two nouns (complex condition) and the second noun phrase (NP2) contained a noun (simple condition) than when NP1 contained a noun and NP2 had two nouns. They argued that, prior to speech onset, more time is dedicated to the conceptual and grammatical encoding of elements within NP1 of an utterance, than to elements in the remainder of the utterance. In other words, sentence production latency depends on the complexity of the first noun phrase of the sentence. The sentence production latency depended on the complexity of NP1, when the complexity of the whole sentence was kept constant. Based on this finding, they argued that conceptual and grammatical planning is not completed for the whole of a sentence prior to the utterance onset. The authors further compared sentence production latencies among four conditions as follows (an example sentence for each condition is given):

(1) Coordinate sentences with the first clause (C1) containing a complex NP1 and the second clause (C2) comprising a simple NP1: *The dog and the foot move up and the kite moves down.*

(2) Coordinate sentences with the first clause (C1) containing a simple NP1 and the second clause (C2) comprising a complex NP1: *The dog moves up and the foot and the kite move down.*

(3) Simple sentences with a complex NP1: *The dog and the foot move up.*

(4) Simple sentences with a simple NP1: *The dog moves up.*

The results showed that the sentence production latency for (1) was the longest, (2) and (3) the second longest, and (4) the shortest. The different latencies between (1) and (2) confirmed the finding of the first experiment. Sentence production latencies were longer before coordinate sentences (1 and 2) than before simple sentences (2 and 4), when the complexity of NP1 was constant. From this finding, the authors argued that some time must be dedicated to planning the second clause prior to sentence initiation. Their argument is contradictory to that of Ford and Holms (1978), that speakers do not plan more than one basic clause ahead. Smith and Wheeldon postulate that the unit of conceptual planning is clausal, whereas the unit of grammatical encoding is phrasal.

Clark and Wasow's (1989) view is in line with Smith and Wheeldon's (1999). Clark and Wasow argued that the amount of information that the speaker wants to convey affects the complexity of the corresponding linguistic units and the difficulty of message encoding, which consequently influences disfluency rates before the constituents. They examined the repetition rates of articles and pronouns in spontaneous speech. They found that the more complex the constituents which follows, the higher the rate. They argued that planning difficulty is affected by the complexity of the constituent. Therefore, the difficulty is hierarchical, not categorical, as Ford and Holms (1978) claimed. It should be noted that the units in question differed in these studies. Ford and Holms (1978), and Ford (1982) considered clauses, whereas Clark and Wasow were concerned with constituents within a clause. Different mechanisms may be at work, when the units differ.

It has been argued that production units tend to be smaller at the stage of articulation than during conceptualisation or linguistic encoding. Sternberg et al. (1978) found that when the participants read the word lists aloud, the number of stressed syllables, rather than the number of words in the list, affects readers' initiation time. Each stressed syllable in the list added 10ms to the initiation time. They proposed that the stress group (a unit consisting of a single stressed syllable and any following unstressed syllables) is the unit of phonological production. Ferreira (1991) found that when the participants were asked to utter sentences after memorising them, the number of stress groups (or "phonological words"), rather than the number of words in the sentence, corresponds to the initiation time. Ferreira reported that the initiation time of memorised sentences was also affected by the syntactic complexity, as measured by the number of nodes in the phrase structure tree. Wheeldon and Lahiri (1997) also argued that a phonological word is a unit of phonological encoding.

### 2.4.2. Frequent locations of disfluencies

Locations with high disfluency rates have been regarded as the points at which most conceptual and linguistic planning takes place. It has been reported that disfluencies are more frequent at discourse boundaries and major syntactic boundaries, such as sentence, clause, and phrase boundaries (Chafe, 1980; Holms, 1988, 1995; Maclay & Osgood, 1959; Shriberg, 1994; Swert, 1998). It has been found that filled pauses, repetitions, and deletions, tend to occur more frequently at the beginning of these units than in the other positions (Clark & Wasow, 1998; Maclay & Osgood, 1959; Shriberg, 1994).

Lounsbury (1954) linked the speaker's cognitive processes with the occurrence of pauses (including filled pauses) and the discourse structure. Lounsbury argued that pauses serve as clues to the strength of association between two linguistic events. According to Lounsbury, longer pauses occur when the transition probability is low. Longer pauses reflect the presence of weak associations between the two linguistic events, and thereby marking the beginning (or the end) of speaker units.

High filler rates were observed at sentence boundaries and clause boundaries both in English and French. For sentence and clause boundaries, respectively, they are about 25% and 3% for English, and about 30% and 8% for French (Ford, 1982; Holms, 1988, 1995).

Chafe (1980) found that disfluencies tend to cluster at the point at which what the speaker talks about widely shifts in narrative. Swerts (1998) reported that filled pauses in Dutch were more frequent at intonational phrase boundaries at which the majority of listeners recognised a paragraph transition, than at other intonational phrase boundaries.

From these findings, it was hypothesised that the deeper the boundary, the higher the disfluency rate. The hypothesis is called *the boundary hypothesis*. Speakers need to choose the contents and the order of the following utterance before formulating linguistic forms. It is assumed that more time is dedicated to conceptual planning at deeper boundaries than at shallower ones. In Section 4.2, this hypothesis is tested by investigating the filler rates at clause, sentence, and discourse boundaries. The results show that filler rates are higher at deeper clause boundaries than at shallower ones, which supports the hypothesis. However, the filler rate at sentence boundaries is not higher than the rate at deep clause boundaries. The filler rate at deeper discourse boundaries is higher than the rate at shallower discourse boundaries in casual presentations. However, this is not the case with academic presentations. It will be argued later on that the degree of spontaneity is likely to affect the filler rates at the boundaries.

It has been reported that the longer and the more complex the constituent which follows, the higher the disfluency rate. As mentioned in the previous section, Clark and Wasow (1998) found that the repetition rates of articles and pronouns were higher when the following constituents were longer and more complex. We call the hypothesis that the more complex the following constituent, the higher the disfluency rate, *the complexity hypothesis*, after Clark and Wasow[3].

Shriberg (1994) found that the more words a sentence contains, the higher the rate at which the sentence comprises disfluencies, particularly at the beginning of the sentence. This finding supports the complexity hypothesis. Watanabe et al. (2004) investigated the rates of filled pauses after four types of case particles in Japanese. Case particles are located at the end of noun phrases (NPs) in Japanese. The authors found that the closer the case tended to be located to the beginning of a sentence, the higher the rate of filled pauses after the case particle. The rate was the highest after topic particles, the next highest after nominative particles, and the lowest after dative and accusative particles. The order of the rates after the four types of case particles corresponded to the order of the lengths and complexities of the following constituents. The results supported the complexity hypothesis.

We test the complexity hypothesis by examining filler rates at sentence, clause, and phrase boundaries as a function of the complexity of the following constituents in Section 4.3. The complexity hypothesis is supported by the filler rates at phrase and clause boundaries. However, the rate at sentence boundaries is not higher than the rate at deep clause boundaries. The results will be discussed in light of speech production models.

It has been pointed out that constituents tend to be longer and more complex when they are preceded by filled pauses, than when they are not. In talks about given topics by 10 subjects, Cook, Smith and Lalljee (1974) found that the number of words in clauses which immediately follow filled pauses was significantly larger than the number of words in clauses not preceded by filled pauses. However, when the same participants described and summarized cartoons without captions, the number of words in clauses after filled pauses was not significantly larger than that in clauses not preceded by filled pauses. The authors speculated that the inconsistent results from the two types of speech were attributable to the difference in syntactic complexity or in the number of samples due to different durations, or the both.

Watanabe et al. (2004) reported that, in academic and casual presentations in Japanese, clauses immediately after filled pauses contained more words than clauses not preceded by filled pauses. This finding agrees with the results of Cook, Smith and Lalljee (1974) from the talks on given topics. Watanabe (2003) carried out a study on Japanese phrases sandwiched between silent pauses longer than 200 ms, or an *Inter Pausal Unit* (IPU). IPUs tend to be smaller than clauses. IPUs contained significantly larger numbers of moras, words, and phrases, when they were immediately preceded by filled pauses than when they were not. These results provided evidence that constituents tend to be longer and more complex when they are preceded by filled pauses than when they are not. In Chapter 5, it is examined through perceptual experiments whether listeners are making use of the tendency that filled pauses are followed by longer constituents in processing speech.

## 2.5. Speech Perception and Disfluencies

Disfluencies go largely unnoticed in everyday communication (Lickley, 1994; Shriberg, 1994). In one's native language, disfluencies seem to be automatically filtered out in speech comprehension processes. The following section contains a review of the literature about the effects of disfluencies on listeners, with particular attention paid to those of filled pauses. Section 2.5.1 surveys studies on the effects of disfluencies on native listeners, and Section 2.5.2 reviews a small body of research on the effects of disfluencies on non-native listeners.

### 2.5.1. Effects of disfluencies on native listeners

Disfluencies have been rather negatively viewed because they seem to interrupt communication and waste time for listeners. However, recent studies have argued that disfluencies can contribute to smooth communication by not only allowing speakers extra time for planning, but also informing listeners of the speakers' mental attitudes or planning difficulties. While listeners are waiting for the speaker to continue instead of taking a turn, they may infer the reason for the speaker's trouble, predict the upcoming utterance, and prepare for it or offer help to the speaker (Clark, 2002; Shriberg, 2005; Stenstroem, 1994). Filled pauses, for example, have been observed to be frequent in dispreferred responses or embarrassing remarks (Finegan, 1994; Rose, 1998; Sadanobu & Takubo, 1995). Such filled pauses are likely to hint at the direction or type of the following utterance and prepare listeners for rather unwelcome remarks.

Filled pauses have also been found to affect listeners' assessments of speakers' utterances. Smith and Clark (1993) pointed out that filled pauses indicate speakers' uncertainties about their answers to general knowledge questions: When speakers provided answers with fillers, they were less confident than when they answered without fillers, and when speakers provided non-answers such as "I don't know" with fillers, they were less confident about not knowing the answer. It was also found that filled pauses are associated with the delay of the answer: the longer the delay, the more likely the speakers are to use fillers. Brennan and Williams (1995) further investigated whether listeners are sensitive to speakers' meta-cognitive states expressed by filled pauses and other devices. They found that listeners evaluated the speaker as 'less confident' when the speaker answered with filled pauses than without delay or with silent pauses of the same duration. These two studies suggest that listeners are sensitive to the speaker's meta-cognitive states expressed by silent and filled pauses, which consequently affect listeners' evaluations of the contents of the utterance.

Other studies have observed that disfluencies affect the language processing of listeners more directly. Fox Tree (1995) examined the effects of false starts and word repetitions on listener comprehension of speech, using an identical word monitoring task. Reaction times were longer when the target words were preceded by false starts than when the false starts were excised, whereas the existence of repeated words before target words did not affect reaction times. The results suggest that false starts disturb listener comprehension of speech, whereas word repetitions have neither positive nor negative effects. Ferreira, Lau and Bailey (2004) provided evidence that the words which were produced in error and then repaired linger and affect parsing.

The findings of Brennan and Schober (2001) indicate that filled pauses between discarded and repairing words such as *uh* in "yel- uh, purple" help listeners compensate for disruptions and delays in speech. Listeners in their experiments responded to repairing words more quickly and accurately when there was a filled pause than when there was a shorter silent pause before the target words. The authors argued that such effects of filled pauses are due to the extra time which elapses during the filled pauses, not their phonological forms, because silent pauses of the same duration had the same effects as the filled pauses.

In contrast with the results of Brennan and Schober (2001), Fox Tree (2002) found that filled pauses at turn beginnings have different effects from those of silent pauses. The participants (overhearers) judged second speakers to have more serious production difficulties when their turns were preceded by a filler, *um*, than when there were silent pauses of the same duration. The results indicate that filled pauses at turn beginnings signal the next speakers' production difficulties more explicitly than silent pauses of the same duration.

Fox Tree (2001) examined the effects of two types of fillers, *um* and *uh*, on listener comprehension in English and Dutch. In both languages, the time needed to monitor target words was shorter when *uh* was present immediately before the words than when *uh* was digitally excised, whereas whether *um* existed or had been removed made no difference in reaction times. The author speculated that *uh* can help comprehension by signalling a short delay and heightening listeners' attention for upcoming speech, whereas *um*, which tends to signal a longer delay, does not have such an effect. These results suggest that fillers with different sound forms may have different effects.

Arnold, Fagnano, and Tanenhaus (2003) found in their experiments using the eye-tracking method that disfluencies, including filled pauses, contribute to reference resolution in discourse. Previous disfluency production studies had shown that disfluencies were more frequent before objects which were newly introduced in the discourse ("discourse-new" objects), than before items which had already been introduced ("discourse-given" objects). Based on these findings, the authors hypothesised that disfluencies bias listeners' expectations toward discourse-new objects. In the experiment, participants were asked to move objects on a computer screen following instructions such as "Now put the candle below the salt shaker," and their eye movements were tracked. The participants fixated their eyes on discourse-new objects longer than on discourse-given items before they had actually heard the target word when the instruction contained disfluencies such as "the" (pronounced as "theee"), and when filled pauses such as *um* or *uh* came before the target word. The results seemed to support the hypothesis. However, the prosody as well as "theee" and *um* in disfluent instructions differed from that in fluent instructions. The adverb, "now" and the verb before the target noun phrase both had wider F0 ranges and longer durations in disfluent conditions than in fluent ones. When the prosodic features in "Now put" and the disfluent features such as "theee um" in the noun phrases were dissociated, neither of the features alone caused discourse-new bias. The authors argued that disfluencies are non-localised speech signals indicating a speaker's production difficulty, and that listeners use multiple cues to assess this difficulty (Arnold, Altman & Tanenhaus, 2003). The results of the two studies indicate that the effects of each disfluent feature are subtle, and multiple cues are necessary for listeners to be aware of speakers' production difficulties and predict the type of the following utterance.

Bailey and Ferreira (2003) found that filled pauses affect listeners' parsing of syntactically ambiguous sentences. When filled pauses were in the pre-nominal positions as in example 1 below, "the deer" tended to be assigned correctly as the subject of the following clause rather than the object of the preceding verb. On the other hand, when filled pauses were in the post-nominal positions as in example 2, "the deer" tended to be assigned as the object of the preceding verb rather than the subject of the following clause. Consequently, the rate at which listeners judged example 1 as grammatical, was higher than the rate at which they judged example 2 as grammatical, although the two cases had the same semantic representations.

example 1) While the man hunted the uh uh deer ran into the woods.
example 2) While the man hunted the deer uh uh ran into the woods.

The authors discussed two possible mechanisms for these phenomena. One was as follows: Filled pauses delay the onset of the disambiguating word, "ran" in example 2. This allows the parser a long time to be committed to the "wrong" analysis, causing the alternative analysis to lose activation and making reanalysis difficult. As a consequence, example 2 is judged ungrammatical more frequently than example 1. In this view, the time between the consecutive constituents is assumed to play a critical role in parsing. The other possibility mentioned was that example 1 is judged grammatical more frequently than example 2 because listeners are making use of filled pauses as cues to a complex constituent, because filled pauses are more frequent at the beginning of complex constituents such as clauses and sentences. As the location of filled pauses in example 1 was in agreement with the tendency of their natural distribution, most listeners correctly judged "the" before *uh* as the beginning of a new clause. In the case of example 2, many listeners are likely to have expected a clause boundary after "deer" because fillers tend to precede clauses. However, as no NP for the subject appeared after fillers, the listeners who failed to reanalyse the sentence seemed to judge it ungrammatical. This analysis assumed that the listeners' parsing is affected by the information of co-occurrences of filled pauses and clause onsets. The authors concluded that both mechanisms seem to be at work, and that filled pauses can affect the parsing of temporally ambiguous sentences.

The results of Arnold, Fagnano, and Tanenhaus (2003) and Bailey and Ferreira (2003) both indicate that listeners are sensitive to the co-occurrence of filled pauses and the type of the following utterance, which consequently affects their on-line speech processing. The former study focused on the discourse status of the referent, whereas the latter was interested in syntactic features of the following constituent. In conversations, we alternate between our roles as speakers and listeners. Therefore, it is plausible to assume that what we do as a speaker affects our behaviour as a listener. In Section 2.4.2, it was pointed out that filled pauses are more frequent before longer and complex constituents. Based on this finding, it was hypothesised that listeners expect a relatively long and complex phrase to follow when there is a filled pause. In other words, it was predicted that filled pauses bias listeners' expectation toward an utterance which is likely to take speakers longer to plan.

In chapter 5, the question whether filled pauses affect listeners' prediction about the contents of upcoming speech is tackled. As mentioned earlier, filled pauses tend to be followed by a long and complex constituent (Watanabe, 2003; Watanabe et al., 2004). If listeners are making use of filled pauses as cues for the content or the syntactic structure of upcoming speech as Arnold et al. (2003a, b) and Bailey and Ferreira (2003) argued, listeners are likely to expect a relatively long and complex constituent when there is a filled pause. This hypothesis is tested through a perceptual experiment with native listeners in Section 5.2, and with non-native listeners in Section 5.3. The hypothesis is supported by the results with native listeners and non-native listeners with high proficiency of Japanese.

**2.5.2. Effects of disfluencies on non-native listeners**

Although it has been claimed that disfluencies are directly relevant to research in foreign language learning and teaching, only a small number of empirical studies have been conducted about their effects on non-native listeners (Buck, 2001; Griffiths, 1991; Rose, 1998). Some researchers have argued that they are the main obstacles to listener perception and comprehension of speech. Voss (1979) asked German subjects to transcribe a stretch of spontaneous English and analysed the transcripts. Voss found that nearly one-third of the perception errors were connected with disfluencies: Misunderstanding was due to either misinterpreting disfluencies as parts of words or misinterpreting parts of words as disfluencies. Fukao, Mizuta, and Ohtsubo (1991) reported that international students studying at Japanese universities had difficulties in coping with disfluencies in lectures: Some students could not distinguish filled pauses from words, and others were not able to comprehend sentences with repairs, omissions or speech errors in lectures.

On the other hand, Blau (1991) claimed that disfluencies can help non-native listeners' comprehension of speech. Blau compared non-native listeners' comprehension of monologues in English under three conditions: (1) speech at a normal speed, (2) speech with extra three second silent pauses, on average, between every 23 words, (3) speech with similar pauses filled with hesitations such as "well," "I mean," and *uh*. In one experiment with Spanish speakers, comprehension scores of the silent pause and the hesitation pause versions were significantly higher than those of the normal version. There was no significant difference between the scores of the silent pause and the hesitation pause versions. In another experiment with Japanese speakers, comprehension scores of the hesitation pause version were significantly higher than those of the silent pause and the normal versions. Blau's study suggests that discourse markers and filled pauses help non-native listener comprehension. However, exactly what made the hesitation pause version the most helpful to listeners is not clear, because neither the duration of the hesitation pauses nor the prosody of the speech surrounding them seem to have been controlled. Positive effects of hesitation pauses may have been due to their longer durations than silent pauses: Silent pauses of the same duration may have the same effects as hesitation pauses. Also, it may have been the prosody of the surrounding speech or the hesitation pauses combined with the prosody that caused the effects rather than the hesitation pauses alone, as disfluencies are likely to be non-localised speech signals (Arnold, Altman, & Tanenhaus, 2003). Given that hesitation pauses themselves facilitated the listener comprehension of speech, whether both discourse markers and filled pauses are helpful to listeners is not clear: Discourse markers may have a positive effect, while fillers may not, or vice versa. Even among discourse markers or filled pauses, some types may be helpful, while others may not, as indicated by Fox Tree (2001).

Summarizing the discrepant results of previous research about the effects of disfluencies on non-native listeners, Buck (2001) argued that disfluencies that slow the speech rate down help the comprehension of non-native listeners as long as the disfluencies are recognised as disfluencies. If listeners fail to recognise the disfluencies as such, they can have detrimental effects. However, as studies with native listeners indicated, word repetitions and fillers, *um*, which slow down the speech rate (measured by the amount of linguistic information conveyed per unit of time), neither helped nor hindered comprehension (Fox Tree, 1995; 2001). Buck's argument needs more empirical support and detailed analyses of various types of disfluencies at different locations.

## 2.6. Chapter Summary

This chapter has surveyed disfluency research relevant to this study. In Section 2.2, we have introduced the types and the features of disfluencies often referred to in the literature and the terminology of disfluency studies. Section 2.3 has surveyed the features of filled pauses in Japanese and some other languages. We have introduced the arguments on whether different types of fillers have different functions. Although some distributional differences have been reported, it is not yet known in what aspect and to what extent their functions actually differ. Section 2.4 has reviewed the speech production models related to disfluency studies. We have pointed out that speech production stages and the units are the focus of such studies, and that disfluencies are regarded as cues for such units. Section 2.5 has surveyed the research on the effects of disfluencies on listeners. The recent research has strongly suggested that disfluencies affect core language comprehension of listeners as well as their assessment of the speaker's attitudes towards the utterance.

**Notes**
1 The rates of fillers, repetitions and deletions are estimated from Figure 23 of Shriberg (1994, p.137).
2 Every basic clause contains one and only one main verb, whether tensed or not, whereas every surface (also called "finite") clause contains one and only one tensed or finite verb.
Basic clause partitioning:
/ I began /working a lot harder / when I finally decided/ to come to Uni.
Finite clause partitioning:
/ I began working a lot harder / when I finally decided to come to Uni. (Levelt, 1989)
3 Clark and Wasow (1989)' s "complexity hypothesis" is as follows: All other thing being equal, the more complex a constituent, the more likely speakers are to suspend speaking after an initial commitment to it. We have modified it for our study.

# Chapter 3

# Speaker Variation in the Use of Filled Pauses

## 3.1. Chapter Overview

It has been reported that frequencies and types of disfluencies widely vary across speeches and speakers. In this chapter, we attempt to find some regularity in the use of fillers across speeches and speakers. This chapter is organised in the following way. Section 3.2 briefly surveys research concerning factors affecting the choice of types of disfluencies. The method of the analyses is described in Section 3.3. Section 3.4 reports the results, which will be discussed in Section 3.5. Finally, Section 3.6 summarises the chapter.

## 3.2. Introduction

As mentioned in Section 2.3.2, Japanese language has quite a few types of filled pauses. However, not much is known about the factors affecting speakers' choice of fillers and other types of disfluencies.

Speech levels[1], individual speakers' speaking styles and characters of disfluencies can be considered as factors affecting speakers' choice of disfluency types.

As we have already surveyed studies about characters of fillers in 2.3, we shortly review disfluency research conducted from sociolinguistic point of view.

Yokobayashi (1994) claimed that Japanese filler, *e*, is typical at the beginning of formal speech. Concerning speaking styles, it is known that speaker variation is large in frequencies and in the types of disfluencies (Inagaki et al., 2002; Shriberg, 1994; Watanabe, 2001). However, some regularity in speakers' use of types of disfluencies has been reported. Shriberg (1994) pointed out that some speakers can be called "deleters" because deletions are more common than repetitions in their speech, whereas others can be called "repeaters" as repetitions are more frequent than deletions. The mean speaking rate of deleters, measured by the number of words per unit time, was higher than that of repeaters. This made the author speculate that deleters need to retract starts as they tend to begin speaking without having planned enough what to say.

Gender and age may affect speaking styles and the choice of disfluency types. It was found both in English and Japanese speech corpora that male speakers produce fillers at higher rates than female speakers (Shriberg, 1994; Maekawa, 2004). Total disfluency rates were also higher for male speakers than for female speakers (Lickley, 1994; Maekawa, 2004).

Shiozawa (1979) observed that the older children grow, the wider the variation of disfluencies, and that frequently used disfluency types change with age. Frequent disfluency types listed in five age groups were as follows:

3–6 year old: *nn, nnto, to*

7–9 year old: repetitions, prolongations of postpositional particles.

10–12 years old: 12 types of disfluencies; *eto, to, nnto, anone, ano, nanka,* (other types not observed)

13–15 years old: 14 types of disfluencies; *e, eto, to, nnto, anone, ano, yappari, nannka,* (other types not observed)

Male speakers in their 20s: prolongations, *e, ano, ma, nanka, soodesune*

Male speakers over 30: *e, ano, ma, sono,* vowel sound fillers

It is regrettable that Shiozawa's research did not give enough information about the number of subjects and situational contexts of the observation.

In the present chapter, we considered the following factors as potentially influential in speakers' choice of disfluency types: speech levels (formal vs. less formal), speaker's gender and age. We investigated the occurrence of fillers and prolongations in speeches compiled in *The Corpus of Spontaneous Japanese* (CSJ) (The National Institute for Japanese Language, 2006). First, we conducted three-way analyses of variance (ANOVA) for seven types of fillers, and inferred the effects of the three factors on the choice of filler types. Second, cluster analyses were conducted to obtain a profile of common combination patterns of fillers across speeches. We will report the analyses in detail in the following sections.

## 3.3. Method

### 3.3.1. Material

We investigated the occurrences of fillers and non-lexical prolongations in two types of presentations, academic and casual, in *The Corpus of Spontaneous Japanese* (CSJ) (The National Institute for Japanese Language, 2006). The corpus contains about 660 hours of spontaneous speeches with 7 million words, 90% of which are recordings of academic and casual presentations. The corpus comprises 987 academic (274.4 hours) and 1715 casual (329.9 hours) presentations with their transcripts and morphological analyses. The academic presentations were recorded at 12 academic conferences, six of which were in fields of engineering, four humanities, and two social and behavioural sciences. Most of the presentations are 12–25 minutes long. The casual presentations (called *simulated public speaking* in CSJ) were given to a small audience in an informal atmosphere by paid volunteers. The speakers talked about general topics such as "the happiest (or the saddest) experience in my life" or "my town" for about 12 minutes on average. The speakers were informed of the speech topic beforehand. They were instructed to make notes for their own speech. The casual presentations are less formal and more like a conversational speech than the academic presentations are, in terms of the length of the sentences, speech rates and the ratio among parts of speech (Maekawa, 2002).

We analysed 240 presentations in total. The classification of the presentations and the number of samples in each condition are given in Table 3–1.

Before sampling the data, we excluded from the analysis the presentations of speakers who had lived abroad for some time between the ages of zero and 12 or those who had lived abroad for more than five years at any age to avoid the possible influence of other languages on the Japanese. We also excluded the presentations which were noted by the recording staff that the speaker was reading out the manuscript, or the presentations with less than ten fillers. After excluding these speeches, we randomly sampled 20 presentations for each condition of the three factors: presentation types (academic and casual), the speakers' gender and age.

The speakers were divided into three age groups: those who were born in the 1950s, 1960s, and 1970s. As the presentations were recorded between 1999 and 2001, we assumed that the year recorded was 2000, and calculated the age of the speakers in that year. As those who were born in the 1950s were between age 41 and 50 in 2000, we call this group the speakers in their 40s, or simply *40s*. Similarly, we call the group born in the 1960s the speakers in their 30s, or *30s*, and those born in the 1970s the speakers in their 20s, or *20s*. As the years of birth of the speakers are separated at five year intervals in the corpus, we assumed the median of the year range as the birth year of a speaker. As the number of academic presentations given by female speakers in their 40s was not enough, three presentations were chosen from those given by speakers born in the second half of the 1940s for this group.

Table 3–1 The classification of presentations and the number of samples

| Speakers' gender | Female | | | Male | | |
|---|---|---|---|---|---|---|
| Year of birth of speakers | 1950s | 1960s | 1970s | 1950s | 1960s | 1970s |
| Academic presentations | 20 | 20 | 20 | 20 | 20 | 20 |
| Casual presentations | 20 | 20 | 20 | 20 | 20 | 20 |

### 3.3.2. The definition and the classification of fillers

As mentioned in Section 2.3.2, the following sounds which have a gap filling function are defined as "fillers," and are given "F" tags in the transcripts in CSJ. The list is given below again. We adopted this definition, and regarded the following sounds with F tags as fillers.

a (:), i (:), u (:), e (:), o (:), n (:), to (:)*, ma (:)*,
u (:) n, a (:) (n) no (:)*, so (:) (n) no (:)*,
u(:) n (t) to (:)*, a (:) (t) to (:)*, e(:) (t) to (:)*, n (:) (t) to (:)*

Notes:
· All types of fillers above followed by *desune* (:) or *ssune* (:) included.
· Fillers with * above followed by *ne* (:) or *sa* (:) included.
· Sounds in parentheses are optional.
· : stands for a long vowel or nasal.

(Koiso et al., 2004)

First, we extracted and counted all the fillers in each presentation. We disregarded the difference in the length of the vowels or the consonants in the transcripts. Thus, *ano* and *anoo*, for example, were regarded as the same type and counted together. We will use the simplest form to express each filler type hereafter: *eto* for any of e (:) (t) to (:) (sounds in parentheses are optional), for example. Based on the frequency of each filler type and their sound features, we made seven categories of fillers as follows: *ano, e, eto, ma, sono*, vowel sounds other than *e* (i.e. *a, i, u, o*) together with a nasal, *n*, and the others. *e* was separated from the other vowel sound fillers because of its far higher frequency than the others. As the cumulative rate of the first six categories amounted to 99% of the total fillers, we excluded the last category, "others", from the analysis. We included non-lexical prolongations of vowels and consonants (tagged as "H" and "Q" in CSJ, respectively) in the analysis instead, because prolongations are assumed to allow speakers time for planning as fillers.

### 3.3.3. Procedure

First, we computed the rates of fillers in total and of the seven categories in each presentation. Then, on each category, we conducted three-way analyses of variance (ANOVA) to examine the effects of the three factors: the speech level, the speakers' gender and age.

Second, we conducted separately the correspondence analyses for the academic and the casual presentations using the frequency data of the seven types of fillers, and quantified each presentation and each type of fillers. Using the scores of the presentations obtained through the correspondence analyses, we conducted cluster analyses by the Ward method and extracted clusters for each presentation type. We inspected the features of each cluster in the two types of presentations.

## 3.4. Results

### 3.4.1. General tendency

Table 3–2 shows the mean frequencies and the mean rates of fillers in total and of seven categories. Figure 3–1 illustrates the rate of each category in the academic and the casual presentations separately. The total rate is higher in the casual presentations than in the academic presentations. Figure 3–1 shows the general tendency that *e* is the most frequent filler in academic presentations whereas prolongations are the most frequent in casual presentations.

Table 3–2 The mean frequencies and the mean rates of seven categories of fillers

|  | *e* | *ano* | *ma* | vowel | *eto* | *sono* | prolongation | Total |
|---|---|---|---|---|---|---|---|---|
| Frequency | 73 | 32 | 30 | 17 | 14 | 10 | 55 | 231 |
| Rate/word (%) | 2.4 | 1.1 | 1.1 | 0.6 | 0.4 | 0.3 | 2.2 | 8.1 |

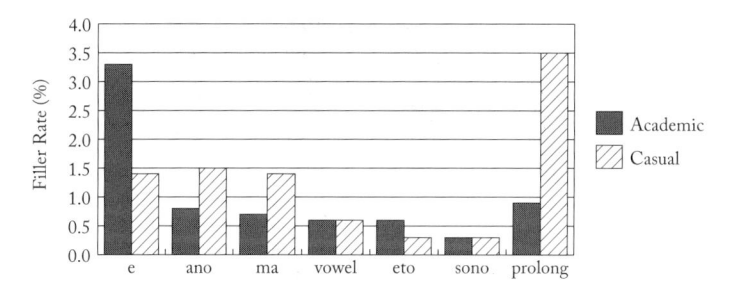

Figure 3–1 The rates of filler type groups in academic and casual presentations

Figure 3–2 indicates the mean rate of fillers in total (prolongations included). A three-way ANOVA showed main effects of presentation type, gender, and age. $F(1, 228) = 21.36, p < .001, F(1, 228) = 29.00, p < .001, F(2, 228) = 5.96, p < .01$, respectively. There was no significant interaction between any factors, presentation type × gender × age: $F(2, 228) = .07, p = .93$; presentation type × gender: $F(1, 228) = 2.02, p = .16$; presentation type × age: $F(2, 228) = 1.78, p = .17$; gender × age: $F(2, 228) = 1.82, p = .16$. Paired comparisons (alpha adjusted by Bonferroni) showed that speakers born in the 1950s (those in their 40s at the time of recording) and those born in the 1960s (in their 30s) use significantly more fillers than the speakers born in the 1970s (in their 20s), but that there was no significant difference between the speakers in their 30s and 40s, 20s vs. 30s: $t(79) = 3.04, p < .01$; 20s vs.40s: $t(79) = 2.94, p < .05$, 30s vs. 40s: $t(79) = 0.10, p = 1.00$.

The total filler rate was significantly higher in casual presentations than in academic presentations, among male speakers than female speakers, and among speakers in their 30s and 40s than those in their 20s.

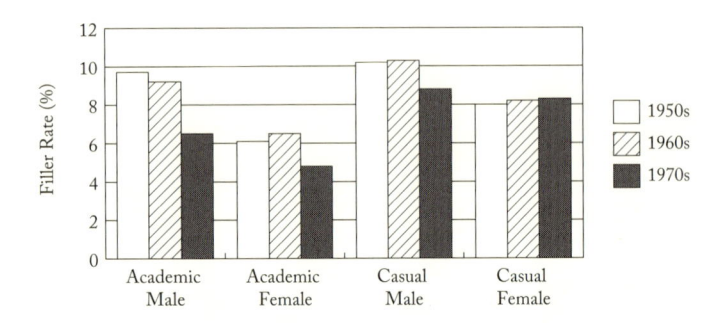

Figure 3–2 The mean rate of fillers in total

### 3.4.2. Features of each type of fillers
#### 3.4.2.1. Features of *e*

Figure 3–3 demonstrates the mean rate of *e* in each group. A three-way ANOVA showed main effects of presentation type and gender as $F(1, 228) = 52.51, p < .001$; $F(1, 228) = 26.67, p < .001$, respectively. There was no main effect of age,; $F(2, 228) = .25, p = .78$. There was no significant interaction between any factors: presentation type × gender × age: $F(2, 228) = 2.11, p = .12$; presentation type × gender: $F(1, 228) = .10, p = .75$; presentation type × age: $F(2, 228) = .59, p = .56$; gender × age: $F(2, 228) = 1.65, p = .20$. *e* rate was significantly higher in academic presentations than in casual presentations, and male speakers produced *e* at significantly higher rates than female speakers.

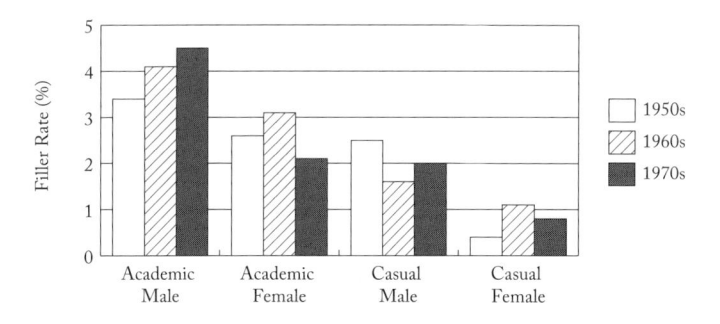

Figure 3–3 The mean rate of *e*

#### 3.4.2.2. Features of *ano*

Figure 3–4 illustrates the mean rate of *ano* in each group. A three-way ANOVA revealed that there were main effects of presentation type and age, $F(1, 228) = 20.78, p < .001, F(2, 228) = 17.78, p < .001$, respectively, but not gender, $F(1, 228) = .09, p = .76$. There was no significant interaction between any factors, presentation type × gender × age: $F(2, 228) = .46, p = .63$; presentation type × gender: $F(1, 228) = .55, p = .46$; presentation type × age: $F(2, 228) = .79, p = .46$; gender × age: $F(2, 228) = .71, p = .49$. Paired comparisons (alpha adjusted by Bonferroni) showed that speakers in their 40s use *ano* at significantly higher rates than speakers in their 30s, and that speakers in their 30s utter *ano* at significantly higher rates than speakers in their 20s, 40s vs. 30s: $t(79) = 2.41, p < .05$; 30s vs. 20s: $t(79) = 3.52, p < .01$, 40s vs. 20s: $t(79) = 5.93, p < .001$.

In contrast with the *e* rate, the *ano* rate was significantly higher in casual presentations than in academic presentations, and older speakers produced *ano* more frequently than younger speakers.

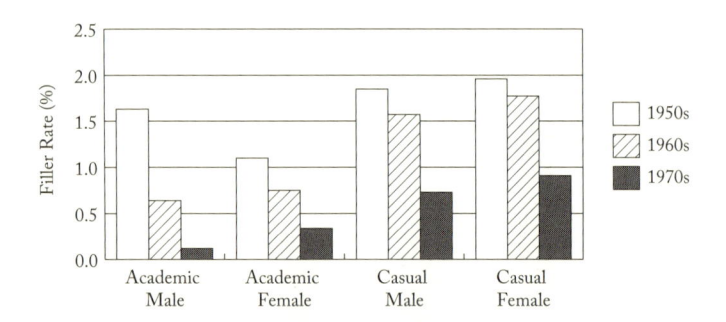

Figure 3–4 The mean rate of *ano*

#### 3.4.2.3. Features of *ma*

Figure 3–5 illustrates the mean rate of *ma* in each group. A three-way ANOVA showed that there were significant interactions between presentation type and gender, and between gender and age, $F(1, 228) = 4.01, p < .05, F(2, 228) = 4.70, p < .01$, respectively. Interactions among the three factors, and between presentation type and age were not significant, $F(2, 228) = .57, p = .57; F(2, 228) = 1.89, p = .15$, respectively.

In both types of presentations, male speakers produced *ma* at significantly higher rates than female speakers, in academic: $F(1, 228) = 2.18, p < .05$; in casual: $F(1, 228) = 5.01, p < .05$. When we inspect presentation factor by gender, male speakers used significantly more *ma* in casual presentations than in academic ones, whereas there was no significant difference in the *ma* rates between the two types of presentations by female speakers, $F(1, 228) = 4.71, p < .05; F(1, 228) = 1.88, p = .06$; respectively.

When we compared the rates between the age groups by gender, there was a significant difference among male speakers, but no significant difference was found among the female speakers, $F(2, 228) = 5.78, p < .01; F(2, 228) = .66, p = .52$, respectively. Paired comparisons (alpha adjusted by Bonferroni) revealed that the male speakers in their 30s produced significantly more *ma* than those in their 20s, but that there was no significant difference between the other groups, 20s vs. 30s: $t(79) = 3.37, p < .05$; 20s vs. 40s: $t(79) = .59, p = .13$; 30s vs. 40s: $t(79) = 2.08, p = .12$. When we look at the gender factor by age, there were significant differences between the two genders in their 30s and 40s, but not in their 20s, 30s: $F(1, 228) = 25.55, p < .001$; 40s: $F(1, 228) = 9.23, p < .01$; 20s: $F(1, 228) = .52, p = .47$. Male speakers in their 30s and 40s produced significantly more *ma* than their female counterparts, but there was no significant gender difference among speakers in their 20s.

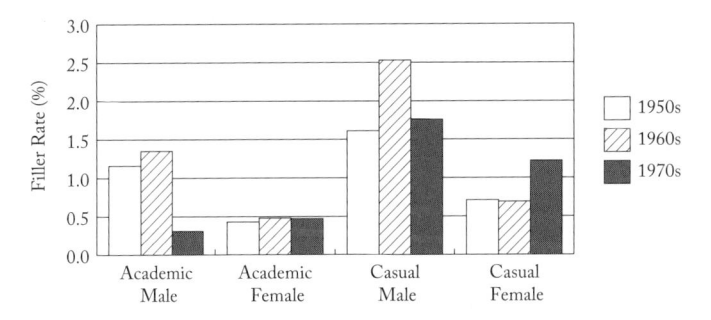

Figure 3–5 The mean rate of *ma*

### 3.4.2.4. Features of vowel type fillers

Figure 3–6 shows the mean rate of the vowel type fillers in each group. A three-way ANOVA revealed that there were significant interactions between presentation type and gender, and between gender and age, $F(1, 228) = 6.54, p < .05$, $F(2, 228) = 3.10, p < .05$, respectively. Interactions among the three factors, and between presentation type and age were not significant, $F(2, 228) = .35, p = .71$; $F(2, 228) = 1.96, p = .14$, respectively.

There was a significant difference in the rates between the two genders in academic presentations, but no significant difference was found in casual presentations, $F(1, 228) = 22.95, p < .001, F(1, 228) = 1.38, p = .24$, respectively. Male speakers used vowel type fillers at significantly higher rates than female speakers in academic presentations, but there was no significant difference in the rates between male and female speakers in casual presentations. When we compared the rates between the presentation types by gender, there was a significant difference among female speakers, but no significant difference was found among male speakers, $F(1, 228) = 5.02, p < .05, F(1, 228) = 1.89, p = .17$, respectively. Female speakers used vowel type fillers at significantly higher rates in casual presentations than in academic ones.

When we compare the rates between the age groups by gender, there was a significant difference among male speakers, but no significant difference was found among female speakers, $F(2, 228) = 8.99, p < .001; F(2, 228) = .44, p = .64$, respectively. Paired comparisons (alpha adjusted by Bonferroni) showed that male speakers in their 40s produced significantly more vowel type fillers than those in their 20s, but that there was no significant difference between the other age groups, 20s vs. 40s: $t(79) = 4.25, p < .05$; 20s vs. 30s: $t(79) = 2.02, p = .13$; 30s vs. 40s: $t(79) = 2.22, p = .08$. When we inspect the rates between the two genders by age, there was a significant difference between the two groups among speakers

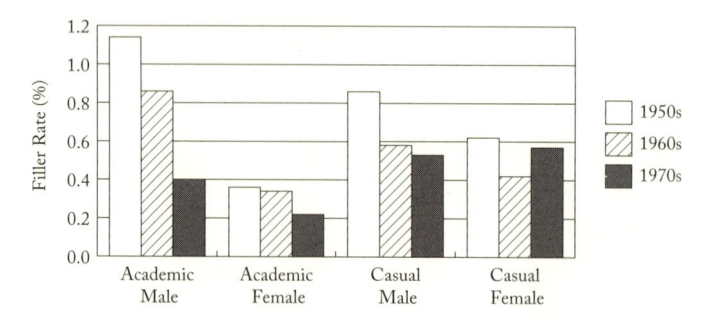

Figure 3–6 The mean rate of vowel type fillers

in their 30s and 40s, but no significant difference was found between the groups in their 20s, 30s: $F(1, 228) = 7.28, p < .01$; 40s: $F(1, 228) = 16.39, p < .001$; 20s: $F(1, 228) = .31, p = .58$. Male speakers in their 30s and 40s uttered significantly more vowel type fillers than their female equivalents, but there was no significant difference in the rates between male and female speakers in their 20s.

### 3.4.2.5. Features of *eto*

Figure 3–7 demonstrates the mean rate of *eto* in each group. A three-way ANOVA showed that there were main effects of presentation type and age, $F(1, 228) = 11.91, p < .001$, $F(2, 228) = 3.86, p < .05$, respectively, but no main effect of gender, $F(1, 228) = .13, p = .72$. There was no significant interaction between any factors, presentation type × gender × age: $F(2, 228) = 0.01, p = .99$; presentation type × gender: $F(1, 228) = .08, p = .78$; presentation type × age: $F(2, 228) = .12, p = .89$; gender × age: $F(2, 228) = 2.58, p = .08$. The rate of *eto* was significantly higher in academic presentations than in casual presentations. Regarding age factor, paired comparisons (alpha adjusted by Bonferroni) showed that there was a significant difference between speakers in their 30s and 40s, $t(159) = 2.69, p < .05$. There was no significant difference between the other age groups, 20s vs. 30s: $t(159) = .74, p = 1.00$, 20s vs. 40s: $t(159) = 1.95, p = .16$. Speakers in their 30s

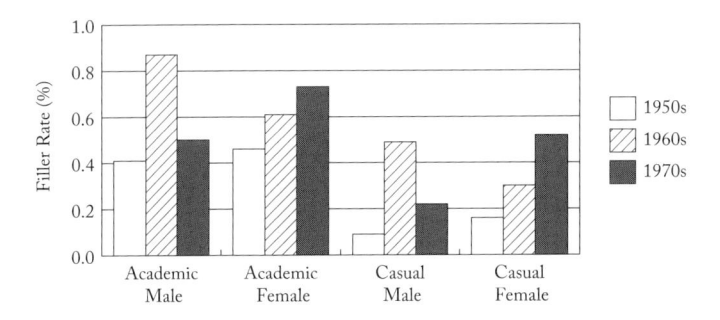

Figure 3–7 The mean rate of *eto*

used *eto* significantly more frequently than speakers in their 40s.

#### 3.4.2.6. Features of *sono*

Figure 3–8 illustrates the mean rate of *sono* in each group. A three-way ANOVA revealed that there were main effects of gender and age, $F(1, 228) = 12.11, p < .001$, $F(2, 228) = 3.11, p < .05$, respectively, but not the presentation type, $F(1, 228) = .13, p = .72$. There was no significant interaction between any factors, presentation type × gender × age: $F(2, 228) = 0.67, p = .51$; presentation type × gender: $F(1, 228) = .12, p = .73$; presentation type × age: $F(2, 228) = 1.47, p = .23$; gender × age: $F(2, 228) = 2.97, p = .05$. Although the main effect of the age factor was significant, paired comparisons (alpha adjusted by Bonferroni) showed no significant difference among the three conditions, 20s vs. 30s: $t(159) = 2.11, p = 0.11$; 20s vs. 40s: $t(159) = 2.20, p = .09$; 30s and 40s, $t(159) = .09, p = 1.00$. *sonos* were used at significantly higher rates by male speakers than female speakers.

#### 3.4.2.7. Features of prolongations

Figure 3–9 shows the mean rate of the prolongations in each group. A three-way ANOVA revealed that there was a significant interaction between presentation type and gender, $F(1, 228) = 4.57, p < .05$. No other interaction was significant.

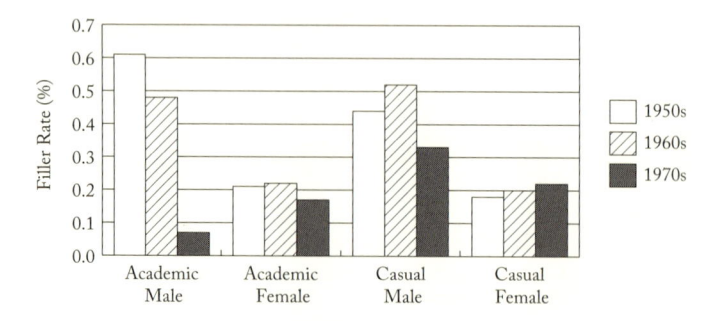

Figure 3–8 The mean rate of *sono*

There was no main effect of age factor, $F(2, 228) = .12, p = .89$. Both male and female speakers used prolongations at significantly higher rates in casual presentations than in academic presentations, $F(1, 228) = 40.91, p < .001, F(1, 228) = 88.69, p < .001$, respectively. Female speakers used prolongations significantly more frequently than male speakers in casual presentations, but there was no significant difference in the rates between male and the female speakers in academic presentations, $F(1, 228) = 8.11, p < .01, F(1, 228) = .03, p = .86$, respectively.

### 3.4.2.8. Section summary

Table 3–3 summarizes the findings. The results of the ANOVA suggest that speech levels and speakers' gender and age affect the frequency and the choice of filler types, and that the influential factors differ depending on the filler type. The speech level is relevant to the use of all the filler types except for *sono*. *e* and *eto* are more frequent in academic presentations, whereas *ano* and prolongations are more common in casual presentations. *ma* is more frequently used in casual presentations than in academic presentations by male speakers.

Speakers' gender seems to affects the use of most filler types, except for *ano* and *eto*. In other words, *ano* and *eto* can be used regardless of the speakers' gender. *e, ma, sono*, and vowel type fillers are more preferred by male speakers, whereas

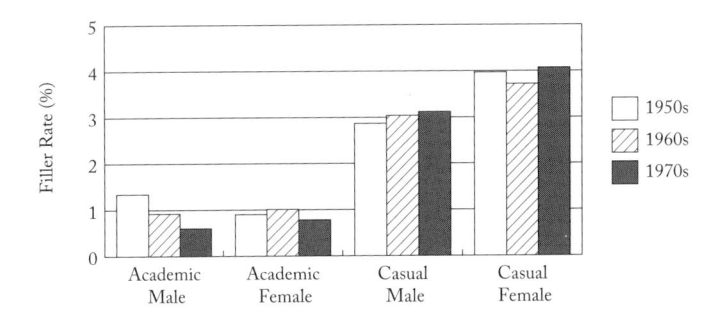

Figure 3-9 The mean rate of prolongations

prolongations are more favoured by female speakers in casual presentations.

Speakers' age is relevant to the use of *ano, eto, ma* and vowel type fillers. *ano* is more recurrent, the older the speakers. *ma* is more common among male speakers in their 30s than those in their 20s. Vowel type fillers are more frequent among male speakers in their 40s than those in their 20s. In contrast, *eto* is more popular among speakers in their 30s than those in their 40s.

In the following section, we will investigate more closely the combination patterns of fillers in the presentations.

### 3.4.3. Results of correspondence analyses
#### 3.4.3.1. Academic presentations

We selected the first four dimensions based on the cumulative proportions of inertia (see Table 3–4). These four dimensions explained 85% of the data distribution. Figure 3–10 shows a symmetric map of the first two dimensions for filler

Table 3-3 Summary of the features of fillers

| Filler Type | Speech level (SL) | Gender | Age | SL × Gender | Gender × Age |
|---|---|---|---|---|---|
| Total | A < C | F < M | 20s < 30s, 40s | | |
| e | A > C | F < M | | | |
| ano | A < C | | 20s < 30s < 40s | | |
| ma | | F < M | | M: A < C | M: 20s < 30s 30s, 40s: F < M |
| vowel type | | | | A: F < M F: A < C | M: 20s < 40s 30s, 40s: F < M |
| eto | A > C | | 30s > 40s | | |
| sono | | F < M | | | |
| prolongations | A < C | | | C: F > M | |

A: academic presentations; C: casual presentations;
F: female speakers; M: male speakers

types. The first dimension explained most distribution of *e* (97%), 40% of *ano*, about 30% of *ma*, *eto*, and *sono*, and 22% of prolongations. The first dimension separated *e* from *ano*, *ma*, *eto*, *sono*, and prolongations, which indicates that the occurrence of *e* and the other five types is complementary. The second dimension explained the distributions of 65% of *eto* and 37% of *ano*. The second dimension set apart *eto* from *ano* in the opposite directions from the origin, suggesting that the use of *eto* and *ano* is complementary. Figure 3–11 is a symmetric map of the first and the third dimensions. The third dimension explained 99.5% of the distribution of vowel type fillers. The third dimension separated vowel type fillers from the others. Figure 3–12 illustrates a symmetric map of the first and the fourth dimensions. The fourth dimension explained the distributions of 66% of *ma* and 15% of *ano*. *ma* and *ano* are placed in the opposite directions from the origin, indicating that their occurrence is complementary.

The cumulative explanatory ratios for *sono* and prolongations were rather low (33% and 25%, respectively), and not as reliable as the others. The cumulative explanatory ratios for the other types were over 90%.

Table 3–4 The proportions of inertia of the first four dimensions for academic presentations

| Dimension | Proportion of Inertia | |
| --- | --- | --- |
| | Accounted for | Cumulative |
| 1 | 0.41 | 0.41 |
| 2 | 0.18 | 0.60 |
| 3 | 0.13 | 0.73 |
| 4 | 0.12 | 0.85 |

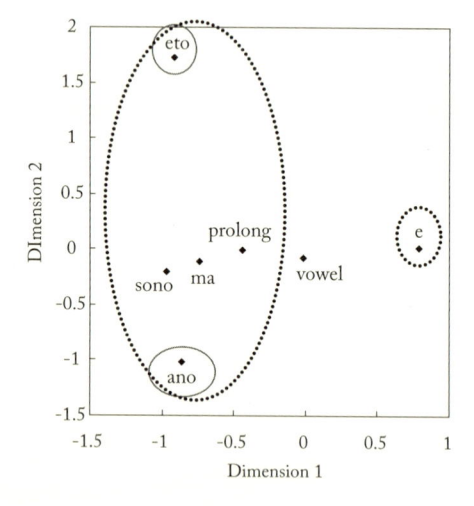

Figure 3–10 A symmetric map of the first and the second dimensions for filler types in academic presentations. The first dimension separates *e* from *ano*, *ma*, *eto*, *sono* and prolongations (indicated by dotted circles). The second dimension sets *eto* apart from *ano* (shown by solid circles).

### 3.4.3.2. Casual presentations

We selected the first four dimensions based on the cumulative proportions of inertia (see Table 3–5). These four dimensions explained 89% of the data distribution. Figure 3–13 shows a symmetric map of the first two dimensions for filler types. The first dimension explained most distribution of *e* (92%), 51% of prolongations, and 14% of *ano*. *e* and prolongations are located in the opposite directions from the origin, indicating that their occurrence tends to be complementary. The second dimension explained the distributions of 87% of *ma*, 18% of *sono*, and about 10% of *eto* and prolongations. *Ma* and *sono* are placed close to each other, suggesting that presentations in which they frequently occur tend to overlap. Figure 3–14 is a symmetric map of the first and the third dimensions. The third dimension explained 79% of *eto* and 19% of *ano*. *eto* and *ano* are located at opposite directions from the origin, indicating that their occurrence tends to be complementary. Figure 3–15 illustrates a symmetric map of the first and the fourth dimensions. The fourth dimension explained the distributions of 65% of *ano* and 34% of prolongations. *ano* and prolongations are placed in the opposite directions from the origin, suggesting that their distribution tends to be complementary.

The cumulative explanatory ratios for *sono* and vowel type fillers were low (23% and 4%, respectively) compared with those of the other fillers (97–100%), and not as reliable as the others.

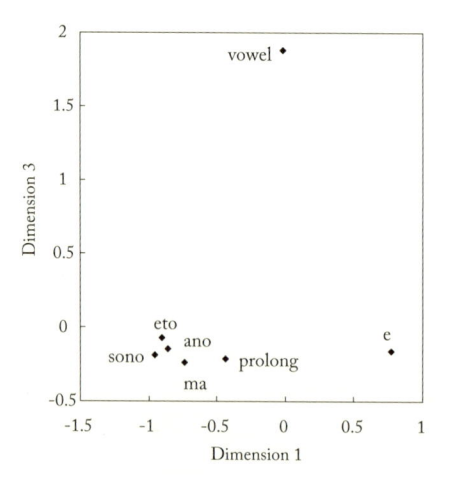

Figure 3–11  A symmetric map of the first and the third dimensions for filler types in academic presentations. The third dimension separates vowel type fillers from the others.

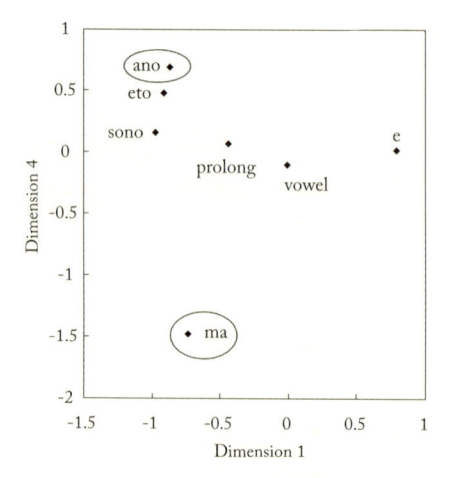

Figure 3–12  A symmetric map of the first and the fourth dimensions for filler types in academic presentations. The fourth dimension sets *ma* apart from *ano*.

Table 3–5 The proportions of inertia of the first four dimensions for casual presentations

| Dimension | Proportion of Inertia | |
|---|---|---|
| | Accounted for | Cumulative |
| 1 | 0.36 | 0.36 |
| 2 | 0.20 | 0.56 |
| 3 | 0.19 | 0.75 |
| 4 | 0.15 | 0.89 |

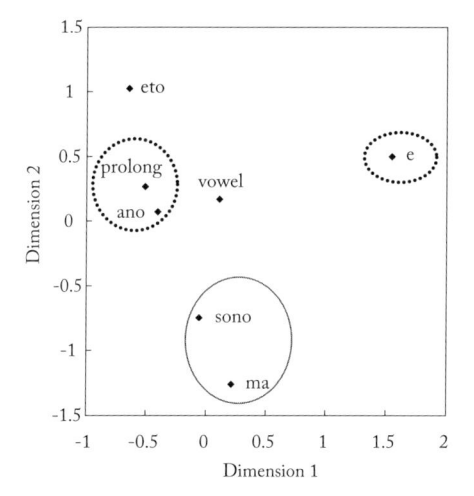

Figure 3–13 A symmetric map of the first and the second dimensions for filler types in casual presentations. The first dimension separated *e* from prolongations and *ano* (indicated by dotted circles). The second dimension set *ma* and *sono* apart from the others (indicated by a solid circle).

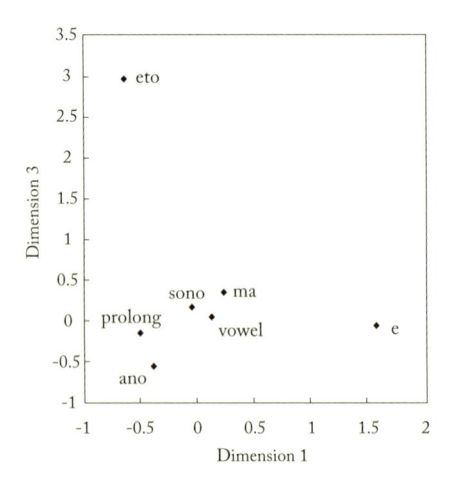

Figure 3–14  A symmetric map of the first and the third dimensions for filler types in casual presentations. The third dimension separates *eto* from the others.

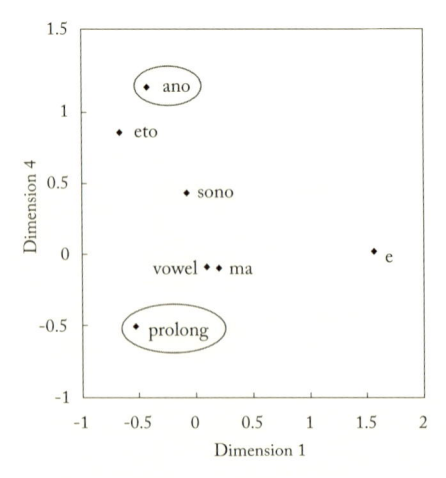

Figure 3–15  A symmetric map of the first and the fourth dimensions for filler types in casual presentations. The locations of *ano* and prolongations indicate their complementary distribution (indicated by circles).

### 3.4.4. Clustering of presentations

Using the four dimension scores of each presentation obtained through the correspondence analyses, we conducted cluster analyses by the Ward method and extracted five clusters in each presentation type. The mean frequency of each type of fillers per 100 words is given in Figure 3–16, for academic presentations, and in Figure 3–17, for casual presentations. We named the clusters after frequent filler types, as shown in Table 3–6 for academic presentations and in Table 3–7 for casual presentations. The number of presentations in each cluster is also given in the tables.

The most frequent fillers in four out of the five clusters (Cluster ID 1–4) were the same in both academic and casual presentations, except that prolongations were slightly more frequent than *ma* (3.2 and 3.0 per 100 words, respectively) in the fourth cluster of casual presentations. However, the frequent fillers in the fifth groups were different. Vowel type fillers and *e* were common in the fifth group of academic presentations, whereas prolongations were dominant in casual presentations. We named the fifth cluster of academic presentations *vowel* group, although *e* were slightly more frequent than vowel type fillers (2.8 and 2.3 per 100 words, respectively).

Figure 3–16 and 3–17 show that *e* is more frequent in all the paired clusters in academic presentations than in casual presentations whereas prolongations are more common in casual presentations than in academic ones. The difference in the fifth clusters revealed that most of the frequent users of vowel type fillers can be found in academic presentations, whereas most of the heavy users of prolongations are in casual presentations. Figure 3–18 illustrates the ratio of each cluster in the two presentation types. The *e* group forms a majority of academic presentations (58%). In casual presentations, the *e* group, the *ma* group and the prolong group show approximately the same ratios (around 30%).

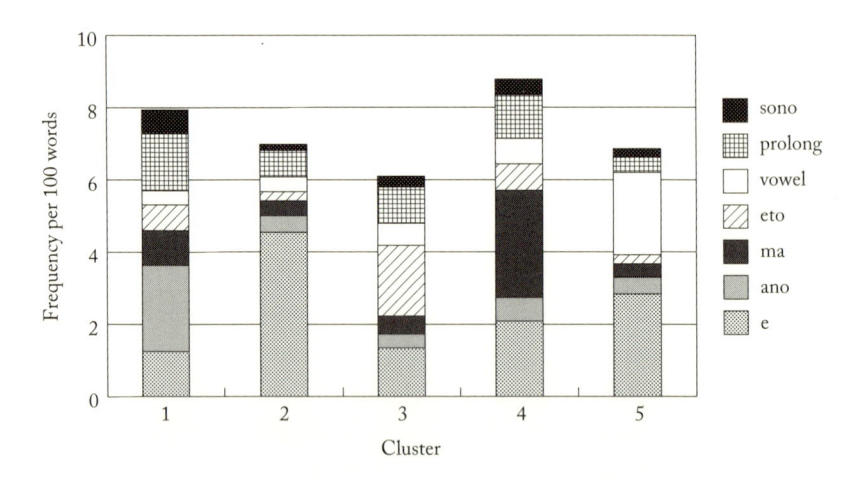

Figure 3–16 The mean frequency of each type of fillers per 100 words in five clusters of academic presentations

Table 3–6 The names of clusters and the numbers of their members in academic presentations

| Cluster ID | 1 | 2 | 3 | 4 | 5 |
|---|---|---|---|---|---|
| Cluster name | *ano* | *e* | *eto* | *ma* | vowel |
| Frequency | 19 | 69 | 17 | 9 | 6 |

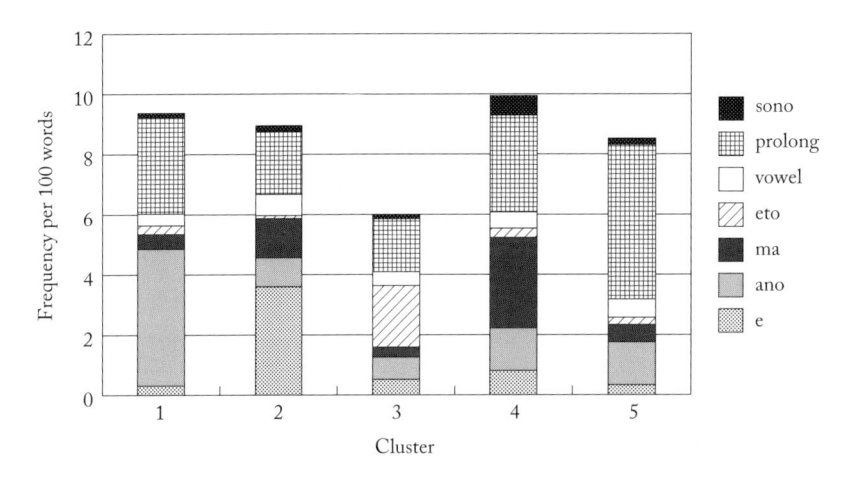

3 Speaker Variation in the Use of Filled Pauses    57

Figure 3–17  The mean frequency of each type of fillers per 100 words in five clusters of casual presentations

Table 3–7  The names of clusters and the numbers of their members in casual presentations

| Cluster ID | 1 | 2 | 3 | 4 | 5 |
|---|---|---|---|---|---|
| Cluster name | *ano* | *e* | *eto* | *ma* | prolong |
| Frequency | 8 | 35 | 5 | 32 | 40 |

|          | ano | e  | eto | ma | vowel |
|----------|-----|----|-----|----|-------|
| Academic | 16  | 58 | 14  | 8  | 5     |

|        | ano | e  | eto | ma | prolong |
|--------|-----|----|-----|----|---------|
| Casual | 7   | 29 | 4   | 27 | 33      |

Ratio of Each Cluster (%)

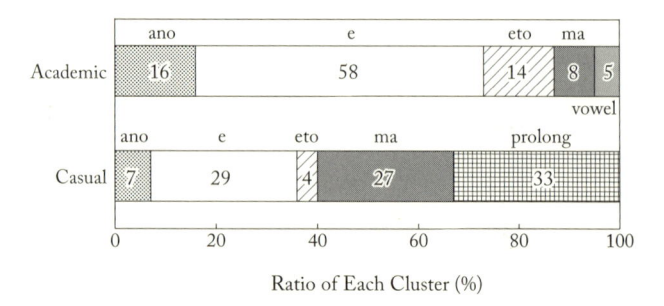

Figure 3–18 The ratio of each cluster in the two presentation types

### 3.4.5. Features of each cluster

Now we examine the combination pattern of fillers in each cluster. In the *ano* groups, prolongations are also relatively frequent in both academic and casual presentations. In the *e* groups, *e* ratio to the total number of fillers is higher in academic presentations than in casual presentations (65% and 40%, respectively). The *eto* groups have the lowest total filler rates, whereas the *ma* groups have the highest total filler rates both in academic and casual presentations. In the *ma* groups, *sono* rates are high compared with the rates in the other groups in both types of presentations. In the vowel group of academic presentations, *e* rate is also high. This means that 75% of fillers used in this group are simply Japanese vowels.

Figure 3–19 and Figure 3–20 demonstrate the ratio of male and female speakers in each cluster, Figure 3–19 for academic presentations and Figure 3–20 for casual presentations. Note that 50% are male speakers in total. The two figures reveal that the majority of the *ano* groups are female speakers while the majority of *ma* groups are male speakers both in academic and casual presentations. Male and female ratios are approximately the same in the *e* group of academic presentations, whereas the male ratio is much higher (74%) in the *e* group of casual presentations. All the members of the vowel group in academic presentations are male speakers. In contrast, the majority (80%) of the prolong group in casual presentations are female speakers.

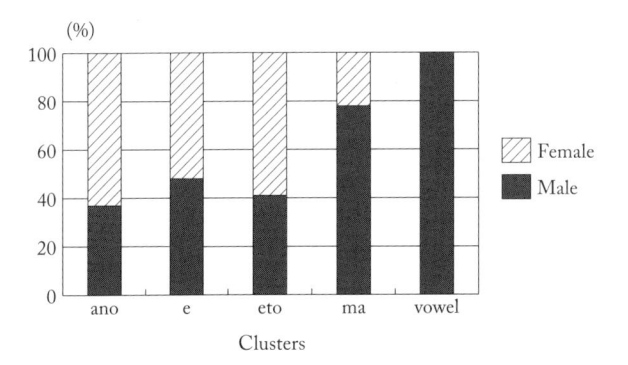

Figure 3–19 The ratio of male and female speakers in each cluster of academic presentations

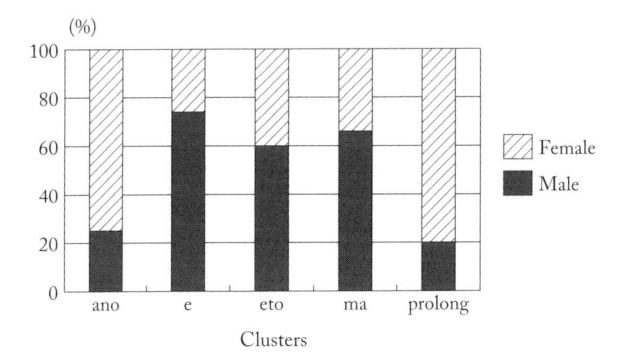

Figure 3–20 The ratio of male and female speakers in each cluster of casual presentations

Figure 3–21 and Figure 3–22 illustrate the ratio of three age groups of speakers, born in the 1950s, 60s, and 70s, in each cluster. Figure 3–21 is for academic presentations and Figure 3–22 for casual presentations. The two figures show that about half of the *ano* groups are those born in the 1950s, whereas the ratio of this age group is small in the *eto* groups. The *eto* groups are composed of younger speakers than *ano* groups. The ratio of those born in the 1950s is also high in vowel group of academic presentations. The results suggest that frequent users of *ano* or vowel type fillers tend to be older than frequent users of *eto*.

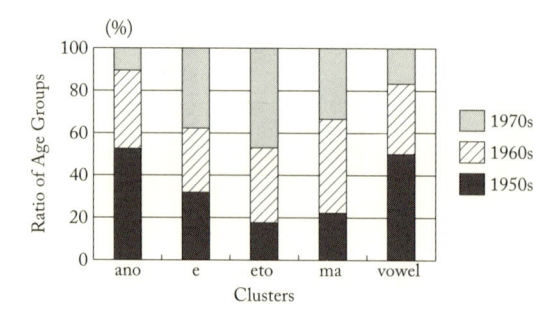

Figure 3–21 The ratio of three age groups (born in 1950s, 60s, and 70s) in each cluster of academic presentations

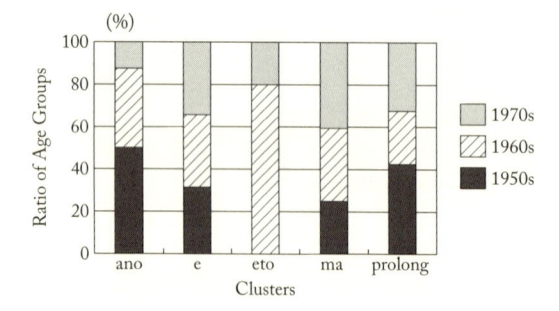

Figure 3–22 The ratio of three age groups (born in 1950s, 60s, and 70s) in each cluster of casual presentations

## 3.5. Discussion

The results of ANOVA have revealed the general tendency in the usage of fillers. Speech levels and speakers' gender and age all affect the total filler rate (prolongations included). The total filler rate was higher in casual presentations than in academic presentations. This result is consistent with previous findings that disfluency rates are lower in more formal settings where careful and clear speech is expected (Broen & Siegel, 1972; Shriberg, Wade, & Price, 1992). It has been reported that filler rates (prolongations not included) are higher among male speakers than female speakers (Maekawa, 2004). Rates of fillers and prolongations are also higher among male speakers than female speakers, although prolongations are more common among female speakers. No previous study has reported that speakers in their 20s (born in the 1970s) produce fewer fillers than speakers in their 30s or 40s. It was reported that disfluencies reduce with pre-planning or rehearsal (Goldman-Eisler, 1968). The lower rate of fillers among young speakers may partly be due to the fact that the majority of speakers in their 20s at academic conferences are post-graduate students and they usually prepare for and rehearse the speech well, as they do not have yet enough experience in presentations. Another possible reason is that young speakers speak more casually and less carefully, particularly in casual settings, than older speakers. Still another interpretation is that speakers born in the 1970s are more fluent than the older generations, and that this tendency of younger speakers being more fluent than older ones, would continue. To test the last hypothesis, real time examinations in the future will be necessary.

Now we turn to the features of each type of fillers. As we have already pointed out in Section 3.2, it seems that speech levels and speakers' gender and age all affect the choice of filler types, and that the influential factors differ according to the filler type. *e* and *eto* were more frequent in formal settings, whereas *ano* and prolongations were more common in casual settings. *e*, *ma*, *sono* and vowel type fillers were more recurrent among male speakers, whereas prolongations were more common among female speakers. Older speakers prefer *ano* and vowel type fillers to *eto*. *eto* are more frequent among speakers in their 30s than those in their 40s.

The results of clustering have shown a profile of five groups of speakers in each presentation type. Four out of the five groups of academic presentations showed similar patterns to those of casual presentations. We named the four groups, *ano* group, *e* group, *eto* group and *ma* group, after the most frequent fillers in the groups. The fifth cluster was characteristic to each presentation type. In academic presentations, there was a group of speakers who used vowel type fillers and *e* very frequently. In casual presentations, there was a large group with high rates of prolongations. Figure 3–23 summarizes the results of the clustering, showing the ratio and the characteristic features of each cluster.

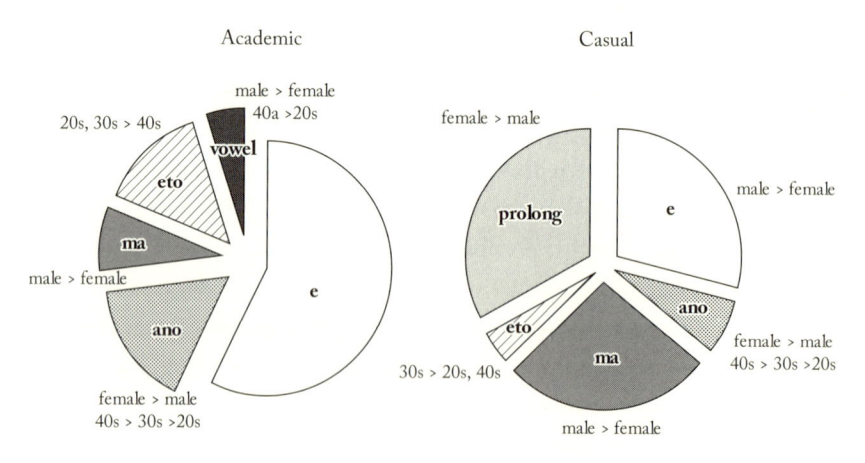

Figure 3–23 The ratio and features of clusters of academic (left) and casual (right) presentations

In academic presentations, *e* group was the majority. As no bias in gender and age was found in this group, *e* seems a typical, neutral filler for formal speech.

It would be safe to recommend international students to use *e,* when they have some trouble in wording during formal presentations. It is interesting to note that the ratio of female members of *e* group decreases in casual presentations. Frequent use of *e* seems to become male biased in casual settings.

Typical perpetual users of *ano* are female speakers in their 40s (i.e. born in 1950s) both in academic and casual presentations. *ano* seems a handy filler for female speakers, because it can be used regardless of the degree of formality. Habitual users of *ano* may decrease in the future, because the members of *ano* groups in their 20s are much fewer than the older members.

The majority of *ma* groups consist of male speakers regardless of the presentation type. It has been pointed out that *ma* is used when one expresses one's opinion modestly. The ratio of *ma* group is smaller in academic presentations possibly because occasions in which one expresses one's opinion are more limited in academic presentations than in casual ones.

Frequent users of *eto* are more likely to be found among speakers in their 20s and 30s, rather than those in their 40s. *eto* seems a filler for younger generations. The ratio of *eto* group is higher in academic presentations than in casual ones. Although it has been pointed out that the use of *eto* in questions or requests can be impolite or inappropriate, the use of *eto* in formal presentations does not seem to be inexpedient. However, as we have investigated only two types of presentations, more kinds of speech should be examined to find out whether *eto* can commonly be used in other formal settings. It is interesting to note that the total filler rate is the lowest in *eto* groups both in academic and casual presentations. *eto* is written as a word of three moras, pronounced as /ɛːto/, in dictionaries (e.g. Niimura, 1998). Most of the other fillers are expressed in less than three moras. The total filler rate is the lowest in the *eto* groups possibly because *eto* tends to be longer and one *eto* allows speakers more time than the other fillers.

A small group of frequent users of vowel type fillers are found in academic presentations. The typical members of this group are male speakers in their 40s.

They frequently use *e,* as well, which means that most of their fillers are simply Japanese vowels.

A group of repeated users of prolongations is extracted only in casual presentations, and it forms the largest group. The majority of the members are female speakers. Lengthening syllables seems the most common strategy for female speakers in casual settings. It is likely to be inappropriate to overuse prolongations in formal speech. Prolongations are in most cases lengthening of vowels. Therefore, they are very similar to vowel type fillers. Whether there is a glottal stop between the vowel and the prolonged part distinguishes vowel type fillers from prolongations. For example, if the last syllable of "kore ga (this SUB)" is pronounced as /ga:/, the last vowel is regarded as one containing prolongation, whereas if the same part is pronounced as /gaʔa:/, the last /a:/ is counted as a vowel type filler. It is interesting that glottal stops differentiate the usage of two similar types of disfluencies quite contrastively, one mainly for male speakers in formal settings and the other rather for female speakers in casual settings. The tense features of glottal stop may be related to formal settings, whereas the lax features of prolongations may be relevant to casual atmosphere in which speakers can be relaxed.

## 3.6. Chapter Summary

We have investigated the correspondence between the rates of seven kinds of fillers and the presentation types and the speakers' gender and age to infer whether such sociolinguistic factors affect the speaker's choice of disfluency types. The results suggest that the speech level and the speaker attributes both affect the choice of fillers, and that the relevant factors differ depending on the disfluency types. The results of this chapter indicate that sociolinguistic factors should be taken into consideration in the study of speech disfluencies.

# Chapter 4

# Speech Planning and Filled Pauses

## 4.1. Chapter Overview

In the present chapter, we test the two hypotheses concerning frequent locations of filled pauses referred to in Section 2.4.2. The first one is **the boundary hypothesis,** which hypothesises that the deeper the boundary, the higher the disfluency rate. The boundary hypothesis is based on the idea that speakers are more likely to need extra time and hence be disfluent, as more conceptual planning is required at deeper boundaries. The second one is **the complexity hypothesis,** which hypothesises that the more complex the following constituent, the higher the disfluency rate. This hypothesis presumes that difficulties in planning constituents are hierarchical as the syntactic structures to be planned have hierarchical structures.

First, we test the boundary hypothesis by examining filler rates at clause, sentence, and discourse boundaries in Section 4.2. Second, we test the complexity hypothesis by examining filler rates at sentence, clause, and phrase boundaries in Section 4.3. Section 4.4 summarises the chapter.

As most disfluency studies have been conducted on English and some other Indo-European languages, it is worth testing these hypotheses with languages such as Japanese, the typology of which is completely different, to find out to what extent the previous findings can be generalised. Studies of different types of languages will shed light on language universals and language specific aspects of speech production and comprehension mechanisms.

## 4.2. Testing the Boundary Hypothesis

As mentioned in Section 2.4, substantial body of studies have claimed that sentences and clauses are speech production units of conceptual and linguistic levels. Disfluency rates at sentence and clause boundaries have been examined to test such assumptions (Chafe, 1980; Clark & Wasow, 1998; Ford, 1982; Ford & Holms, 1978; Holms, 1988). In the present section, we examine filler rates at clause, sentence, and discourse boundaries, to test the boundary hypothesis.

**4.2.1. Adverbial clauses in Japanese**

In Japanese, unlike English and other Indo-European languages, adverbial clauses are marked either by connective particles located at the end of the clauses or by certain conjugations of verbs, adjectives or copula markers. As Japanese is a SOV language, verbs always come at the end of a clause. The order of the clauses in a sentence containing an adverbial clause is shown below. Adverbial clauses always precede main clauses.

(adverbial clause <connective particle>) (main clause).

In spontaneous speech, it is common to observe adverbial clauses successively appearing one after another, without completing a full sentence.

Adverbial clauses are classified into three groups according to the degree of dependency on the main clauses determined by the type of connectives (Minami, 1974). *Type A* clauses are the most dependent on the main clauses. Grammatically, they can have neither topics nor subjects on their own. The topics and the subjects of the main clauses are automatically their topics and subjects. They cannot have their own tense, either. *Type B* clauses can contain subjects on their own, but not topics. *Type C* clauses can have both topics and subjects on their own. Therefore, *Type C* clauses are the most independent of the main clauses. Consequently, it is assumed that boundaries between *Type C* and the main clauses are deeper than the boundaries between *Type A* or *Type B* and the main clauses, and that boundaries between *Type B* and the main clauses are deeper than the boundaries between *Type A* and the main clauses (we will call the three type of boundaries *Type A*, *Type B* and *Type C* boundaries, hereafter). Therefore, it is predicted from the boundary hypothesis that filler rates are highest at *Type C* boundaries, lowest at *Type A* boundaries and in between at *Type B* boundaries. We put sentence boundaries in consideration, as well. As sentence boundaries are assumed to be deeper than clause boundaries, we predict that filler rates at sentence boundaries are higher than those at *Type C* clause boundaries.

It is also known that the three types of clauses compose a hierarchical structure. *Type C* clauses can contain all the three types of clauses, whereas *Type B* can include *Type A* and *Type B*, but not *Type C*. *Type A* can contain only *Type A* clauses. Features of the three clause types are summarized in Table 4–1. Details of the classification system of clause types will be given in Section 4.2.2.2.

Table 4–1 Features of three clause types - whether the clauses can contain their own topics, subjects, and clauses. Plus indicates positive and minus indicates negative.

|  | Own Topic | Own Subject | Containable Clauses |
|---|---|---|---|
| *Type A* | - | - | A |
| *Type B* | - | + | A, B |
| *Type C* | + | + | A, B, C |

### 4.2.2. Method

#### 4.2.2.1. Material

We analysed 177 academic and casual presentations in "the Core" in CSJ (regarding the Corpus, refer to Section 3.3.1). The Core is a true subset of CSJ which contains more detailed and precise linguistic annotations than the other part of the corpus. The speakers of the core are all native speakers of Tokyo Japanese. Three presentations were excluded from analysis because the recording staff of the presentation noted that the speaker was reading a manuscript. Thus, 174 presentations (68 academic and 106 casual) were retained for further analysis.

#### 4.2.2.2. Classification of clause types

In CSJ, three types of tags are provided to sentence and clause boundaries. Correspondence between the traditional clause type classification and the classification system of CSJ is shown in Table 4–2. Boundaries after sentence final forms are labelled as *absolute boundaries*; boundaries after clauses roughly equivalent to *Type C* clauses are labelled as *strong boundaries*; boundaries after clauses roughly equivalent to *Type B* clauses are labelled as *weak boundaries*. *Type A* clauses are not treated as clauses as they are not regarded as units self-contained enough to be treated as such, and therefore no tags are given. Another divergence from the traditional classification system is when auxiliary verbs expressing politeness such as "desu," "masu" are used before *Type B* connectives or when conjunctions follow *Type B* connectives. In these cases, the boundaries are labelled as *strong boundaries* instead of *weak boundaries* (Takanashi et al., 2003; 2004).

We adopted the classification system proposed by Minami (1974), modified by Noda (1986) and Takubo (1987). Some connectives are not classified solely to one type of system. In such cases we have chosen a default group considering the frequency. We adopted CSJ's modification about the polite auxiliary verbs, and tagged *Type B* connective as *Type C* when such auxiliaries existed. We named clauses with sentence final forms *Type D*. The classification of clause types (identified by the connective particles or conjugations) employed in the present study is given in Table 4–3.

Table 4–2 Correspondence between clause boundaries based on traditional clause classification and the classification system of CSJ

| Traditional | CSJ |
| --- | --- |
| Boundary after *Type A* clause | - |
| Boundary after *Type B* clause | weak boundary |
| Boundary after *Type C* clause | strong boundary |
| Boundary after sentence final forms | absolute boundary |

### 4.2.3. Procedure

First, we labelled clause boundaries according to the classification system. Second, we computed the rate of filled pauses at each type of clause boundaries for each presentation. Conjunctions and word fragments at the beginning of clauses were not regarded as parts of the clauses. Therefore, filled pauses immediately after them were counted as fillers at clause boundaries. We compared mean rates of filled pauses at different boundary types.

Table 4–3  Classification of clause types employed in the present study

| Type | Connective or Conjugation | Meaning, Usage |
|---|---|---|
| A | ~nagara, ~tutu | expresses accompanying actions |
|   | ~mama | expresses continuous accompanying actions |
|   | ~tari | lists actions or situations |
| B | ~to, ba, tara, nara | when ~, if ~ |
|   | ~te (wa) | ~ and |
|   | ~te kara | since ~, after~ |
|   | ~te mo | even if ~ |
|   | ~yoo ni | so that ~ |
|   | adverbial form | ~ and |
| C | ~kara, ~node | as ~ (reason) |
|   | ~noni, ~ke(re)do | though ~ |
|   | ~ga | although ~, ~but |
|   | ~si | ~ and (list similar actions or features) |
|   | ~de | ~ and |
|   | ~masite, ~desite | ~ auxiliary verb expressing politeness + and |
| D | yo, ne, to | sentence-final particles |
|   | desu, masu, ta, n | sentence-final forms |

### 4.2.4. Results

Mean frequencies of four types of clauses are given in Table 4–4. As the number of *Type A* clauses was small (4 per presentation on average), *Type A* clauses were excluded from the analysis hereafter and treated as adverbial phrases.

Table 4–4  Mean frequencies of four types of clauses

|  | Type A | Type B | Type C | Type D | Total |
|---|---|---|---|---|---|
| Mean Number of Clauses | 4 | 59 | 56 | 61 | 179 |

Mean rates of the three types of clause boundaries with filled pauses are shown in Figure 4–1. Repeated measures analysis of variance (ANOVA) revealed that there was a significant difference among the filler rates in three conditions, $F(2, 346) = 80.39, p < .001$. Paired comparisons (adjusted by Bonferroni) showed that filler rates at *Type C* and *Type D* boundaries were significantly higher than those at *Type B* boundaries, but that there was no significant difference between the rates at *Type C* and *Type D* boundaries, B vs. C: $t(174) = 13.26, p < .001$; B vs. D: $t(174) = 9.39, p < .001$; C vs. D: $t(174) = 1.27, p = .61$.

Figure 4–2 illustrates mean rates of three types of clause boundaries with fillers in academic and casual presentations, separately. Two-way analysis of variance (ANOVA) with boundary type as within-subject factor and with presentation type as between-subject factor shows main effects of the two factors, boundary type: $F(2, 344) = 83.13, p < .001$; presentation type: $F(1, 172) = 14.98, p < .001$. There was no significant interaction between the two factors, $F(2, 344) = 2.57, p = .08$. Although filler rate was by 10% higher in academic presentations than in casual presentations, the rates at *Type C* and *Type D* boundaries were higher than at *Type B* boundaries and there was no significant difference between the rates at *Type C* and *Type D* boundaries in the both kinds of presentations, academic: B vs. C: $t(67) = 8.85, p < .001$; B vs. D: $t(67) = 6.50, p < .001$; C vs. D: $t(67) = 1.51, p = .36$, casual: B vs. C: $t(105) = 10.31, p < .001$; B vs. D: $t(105) = 6.81, p < .001$; C vs. D: $t(105) = .39, p = 1.00$.

### 4.2.5. Discussion

The rates of filled pauses at *Type C* and *Type D* boundaries were significantly higher than the rate at *Type B* boundaries, which supported the boundary hypothesis. However, the filler rates at sentence boundaries were not higher than those at *Type C* boundaries, which did not support the hypothesis. Sentence boundaries are assumed to be stronger than clause boundaries and therefore the filler rates should have been higher according to the hypothesis. The results indicate that the boundary hypothesis holds true at clause boundaries within a sentence, but not across sentence boundaries.

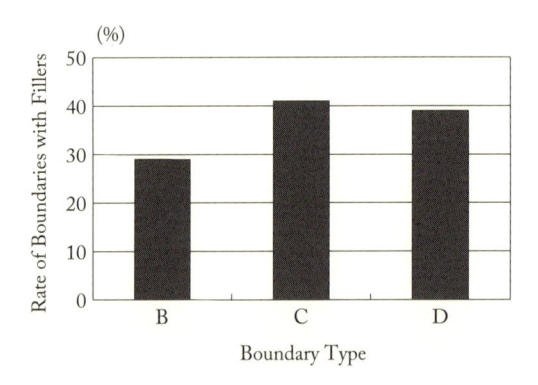

Figure 4–1  Mean rates of three types of clause boundaries with filled pauses (%)

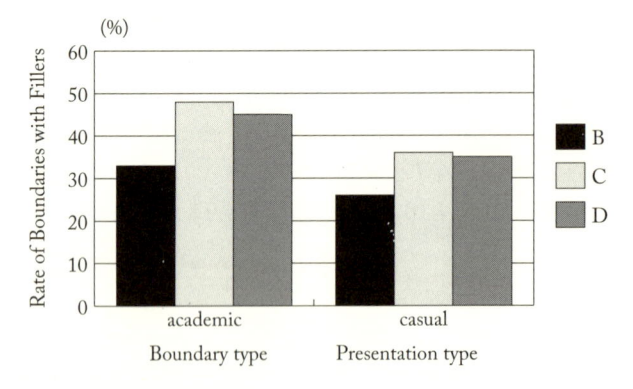

Figure 4–2  Rate of boundaries with fillers in academic and casual presentations

Several interpretations of the results are possible here. One is that after sentence final forms, i.e. at sentence boundaries, it is not unnatural to keep silent for a longer period than at clause boundaries. Therefore, speakers may be preparing for the next utterance without producing filled pauses. Another possibility is that speakers employ different strategies to gain time at sentence boundaries. For example, they may be using conjunctions in place of fillers, because conjunctions can be uttered by speakers without exactly knowing what to say next. The third interpretation is that filler rates of *Type C* and *Type D* boundaries did not make a difference because there is hardly any difference in strengths of boundaries between *Type C* clause boundaries and sentence boundaries in spontaneous speech. In other words, *Type C* clauses may be as independent as simple sentences and have sentence-like properties, as Noda (1986) claimed.

The first possibility is not testable, because there are usually silent pauses at sentence boundaries (so-called "juncture pauses") and there is no knowing which part of the silence is being used for planning the following speech. On the other hand, we can test the second hypothesis by comparing rates of conjunctions at *Type C* and *Type D* boundaries. Regarding the third hypothesis, we employ silent pause durations at the boundaries as a criterion for boundary strengths because it has been reported that longer pauses correspond to deeper boundaries (Hakoda & Sato, 1975; Kaiki & Sagisaka, 1996). We compare silent pause durations between *Type C* and *Type D* boundaries. The procedures and the results of the experiments to test the two hypotheses are reported in the following sections.

### 4.2.6. Rate of clause boundaries with conjunctions
#### 4.2.6.1. Method
The rate of each type of boundaries with conjunctions was computed for each presentation and averaged over presentations. When fillers preceded conjunctions at the boundaries, the boundaries were counted as those with conjunctions.

**4.2.6.2. Results and discussions**

Table 4–5 indicates the rates of three types of clause boundaries with conjunctions. Repeated measures analysis of variance (ANOVA) revealed that there was a significant difference among the rates of three types of boundaries with conjunctions, $F(2, 346) = 544.68$, $p < .001$. Paired comparisons (adjusted by Bonferroni) showed that the rate of *Type D* boundaries with conjunctions was significantly higher than the rates of *Type B* and *Type C* boundaries, and that the rate of *Type C* boundaries with conjunctions was significantly higher than that of *Type B* boundaries, *Type D* vs. *Type B*: $t(174) = 26.96$, $p < .001$, *Type D* vs. *Type C*: $t(174) = 21.01$, $p < .001$, *Type C* vs. *Type B*: $t(174) = 13.30$, $p < .001$.

The results revealed that *Type D* (i.e. sentence) boundaries were followed by conjunctions at significantly higher rates than clause boundaries. The results indicate that the filler rate at *Type D* boundaries was not higher than the rate at *Type C* boundaries because frequent conjunctions, as well as filled pauses, allowed speakers time for planning the following constituents. In other words, conjunctions seem to be playing a role similar to that of filled pauses at sentence and clause boundaries. It is interesting to note that the rate of clause boundaries with conjunctions correspond to the assumed clause boundary strengths. The rate of boundaries with conjunctions may be used as one of the criteria to estimate clause boundary strength.

Table 4–5  Mean rates of three types of clause boundaries with conjunctions (%)

| *Type B* | *Type C* | *Type D* |
|---|---|---|
| 1 | 10 | 41 |

Figure 4–3 illustrates the rates of three types of boundaries with fillers or with conjunctions at the beginning of the following clause. The figure demonstrates that the deeper the boundary the higher the rate of boundaries with fillers or conjunctions. Repeated measures analysis of variance (ANOVA) revealed a

significant difference among the rates of three types of boundaries with fillers or conjunctions, $F(2, 346) = 454.49, p < .001$. Paired comparisons (adjusted by Bonferroni) showed that the rate of *Type D* boundaries with fillers or conjunctions was significantly higher than the rates of *Type B* and *Type C* boundaries, and that the rate of *Type C* boundaries with fillers or conjunctions was significantly higher than that of *Type B* boundaries, *Type D* vs. *Type B*: $t(174) = 28.40$, $p < .001$, *Type D* vs. *Type C*: $t(174) = 12.87, p < .001$, *Type C* vs. *Type B*: $t(174) = 19.72, p < .001$. The results indicate that conjunctions as well as fillers allow speakers time for planning at stronger boundaries.

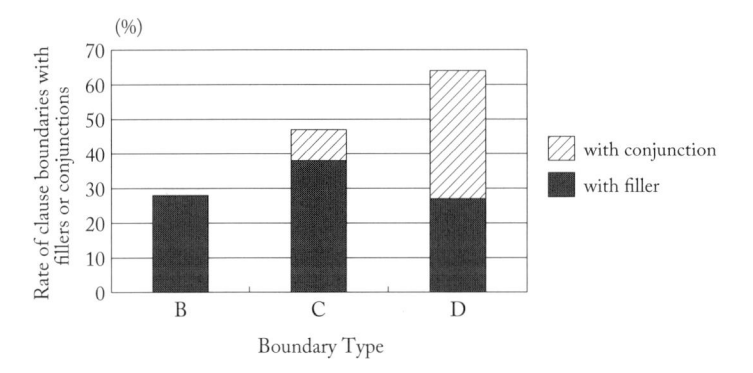

Figure 4–3 Rate of clause boundaries immediately followed by fillers or conjunctions

### 4.2.7. Duration of silent pauses at clause boundaries

When there is only a silent pause at a boundary, we do not know whether the pause is to indicate the boundary or for the speaker to plan speech. However, if there are fillers after silent pauses, we can assume that the preceding silent pause is mainly to indicate the boundary and that the following fillers are for speech planning. Based on this assumption, we measured the durations of silent pauses followed by fillers with or without preceding conjunctions. If durations of silent pauses at *Type C* and *Type D* boundaries do not significantly differ, the *Type C* boundaries are likely to be as strong as *Type D* boundaries. If durations of silent pauses at *Type D* boundaries are longer than those at *Type C* boundaries, *Type D* boundaries are likely to be stronger than *Type C* boundaries.

#### 4.2.7.1. Method
We measured durations of silent pauses before fillers at *Type B, C,* and *D* boundaries ("the disfluent condition"). We also measured durations of silent pauses not followed by fillers at the three types of boundaries ("the fluent condition"). We took the median of the silent pause durations at each type of boundary in each condition for each presentation, and compared mean medians between the conditions.

#### 4.2.7.2. Results and discussion
Figure 4–4 illustrates mean silent pause durations after *Type B, C,* and *D* boundaries in the fluent and the disfluent conditions. Two-way repeated measures analysis of variance (ANOVA), with fluency (whether the silent pause was followed by fillers or not) as one factor and with the boundary type as the other, showed that there were significant main effects of fluency factor, $F(1, 173) = 437.92$, $p < .001$, and boundary type factor, $F(2, 346) = 357.02$, $p < .001$. An interaction between the two factors was also significant, $F(2, 346) = 7.6$, $p < .001$. First, we compared the pause durations among different boundary types in each fluency condition. In both fluent and disfluent conditions, there were significant differences among pause durations in three boundary types. Paired comparisons (adjusted by Bonferroni) revealed that, in both fluent and disfluent conditions, silent pauses at *Type D* boundaries were significantly longer than those at *Type B* and *Type C* boundaries, and silent pauses at *Type C* boundaries were significantly longer than those at *Type B* boundaries: in the fluent condition; *D* vs. *B*: $t(173) = 22.23$, $p < .001$; *D* vs. *C*: $t(173) = 13.57$, $p < .001$; *C* vs. *B*: $t(173) = 15.10$, $p <$

.001, in the disfluent condition; $D$ vs. $B$: $t$ (173) = 17.43, $p$ < .001; $D$ vs. $C$: $t$ (173) = 13.02, $p$ < .001; $C$ vs. $B$: $t$ (173) = 8.12, $p$ < .001. Second, we compared the pause durations between the fluency conditions in each clause type. In all the boundary types, silent pauses in the disfluent condition were significantly longer than those in the fluent condition, *Type B*: $t$ (173) = 17.40, $p$ < .001; *Type C*: $t$ (173) = 12.30, $p$ < .001; *Type D*: $t$ (173) = 11.28, $p$ < .001.

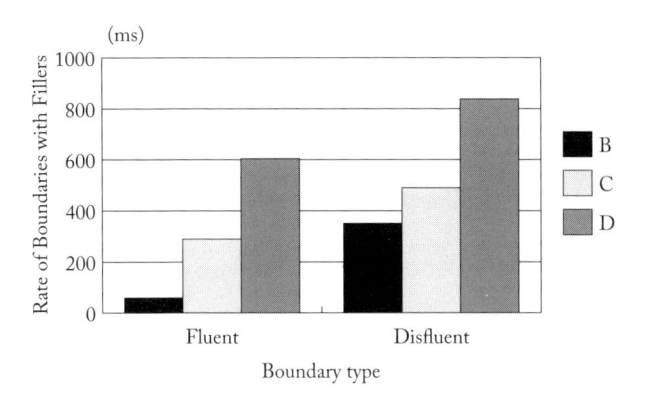

Figure 4–4 Mean silent pause durations at three types of boundaries in fluent and disfluent conditions

Silent pause durations at *Type D* boundaries were significantly longer than those at *Type C* boundaries in both fluent and disfluent conditions. In terms of silent pause durations, there was a clear difference between *Type C* and *Type D* boundaries, as well as between *Type B* and *Type C* boundaries. The results indicate that *Type D* (sentence) boundaries are deeper boundaries than *Type C* as well as *Type B* boundaries, not only in written texts but also in spontaneously spoken texts. The results were against the third hypothesis that *Type C* boundaries are as strong as *Type D* boundaries in spontaneous speech. It is interesting to note that the assumed clause boundary strengths, based on classification of clause types in written texts, clearly correspond to silent pause durations at the boundaries in both fluent and disfluent conditions. It is also worth noting that silent pause durations were longer when they were followed by fillers than when they were not at any given boundary type, which suggests that speakers start planning the following parts of speech some time before starting to utter fillers.

### 4.2.8. Filler rate at discourse segment boundaries

Chafe (1980) reported that disfluencies tend to cluster at the point at which what the speaker talks about widely shifts in narratives. Swerts (1998) found that filled pauses were more frequent at deeper discourse boundaries than at other intonational phrase boundaries. In this section we examine filler rate at discourse segment boundaries to examine whether fillers are frequent at such locations in Japanese.

#### 4.2.8.1. Definition of discourse segment boundaries

We used two types of discourse segment boundary tags contained in forty presentations (15 academic and 25 casual presentations) in the Core in CSJ. The tags were given in the following way.

Three labellers independently divided each presentation into 5 to 15 segments, and described the speaker's purpose of stating each segment. Clause boundaries at which two out of three labellers marked a boundary are regarded as main discourse segment boundaries. We call them "main boundaries (main)". Apart from the labelling by three labellers, the authors of Takeuchi et al. (2004) divided each presentation into segments through discussion. These segments were assumed to be components of larger discourse units delimited by main boundaries. We call the boundaries between the segments that Takeuchi et al. defined "sub boundaries (sub)". We regard main boundaries as stronger than sub boundaries because the units delimited by main boundaries contain the segments. Therefore, filler rate at main boundaries is expected to be higher than the rate at sub boundaries.

It is also predicted from the boundary hypothesis that filler rate at sub boundaries is higher than the rate at clause boundaries, as discourse segments between sub boundaries contain several inter-related clauses. Thus, sub boundaries are assumed to be stronger than clause boundaries.

#### 4.2.8.2. Method

We excluded two presentations from analysis because frequencies of fillers of them were extremely low (three in total for each). Thus 38 presentations (14 academic and 24 casual presentations) were retained for further analysis. We computed filler rates at main boundaries, at sub boundaries which did not coincide with main boundaries, and at *Type C* and *Type D* clause boundaries which did not coincide with sub boundaries in each presentation. Mean filler rates at three types of boundaries were compared.

#### 4.2.8.3. Results

Figure 4–5 illustrates filler rates at *Type C* and *Type D* clause boundaries, sub boundaries, and main boundaries. One-way repeated measures analysis of variance (ANOVA) showed a main effect of the boundary type, $F(2,72) = 5.66$, $p < .01$. Paired comparisons (adjusted by Bonferroni) revealed that the filler rate at main boundaries was significantly higher than the rate at clause boundaries, $t(36) = 4.05$, $p < .001$. The difference between the rates at sub boundaries and main boundaries was marginal, $t(36) = 2.37$, $p = .07$. There was no significant difference between the rates at clause boundaries and sub boundaries, $t(36) = .07$, $p = 1.00$.

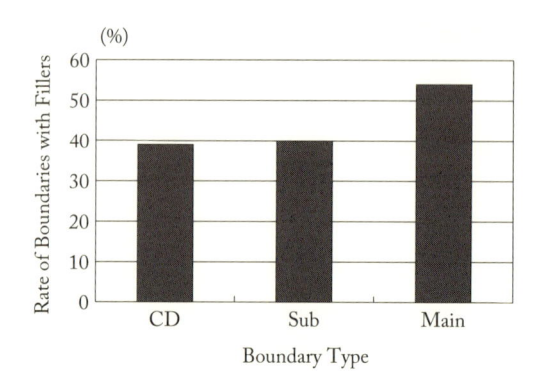

Figure 4–5 Rate of clause and discourse boundaries with fillers

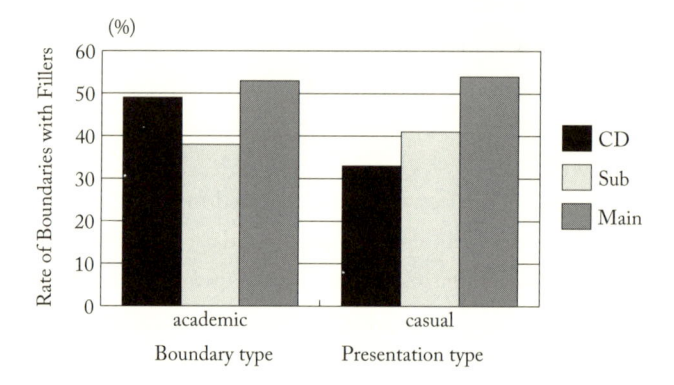

Figure 4–6 Filler rate at clause and discourse boundaries in academic and casual presentations

Figure 4–6 illustrates filler rates at *Type C* and *Type D* clause boundaries, sub boundaries, and main boundaries in academic and casual presentations separately. Two-way analysis of variance (ANOVA) with the boundary type as a within-subjects factor and with the presentation type as a between-subjects factor showed a main effect of the boundary type, $F(2,70) = 4.76, p < .05$, but no main effect of the presentation type, $F(1,35) = .29, p = .59$. An interaction between the two factors was not significant, $F(2,70) = 2.15, p = .14$.

### 4.2.8.4. Discussion

Filler rate at main discourse segment boundaries was significantly higher than *Type C* and *Type D* boundaries, which supported the boundary hypothesis. However, filler rate at sub boundaries was neither significantly higher than the rate at clause boundaries nor lower than the rate at main boundaries. The results indicate that filler rates is higher than the rate at *Type C* and *Type D* clause boundaries only at locations at which topic transition is obvious to majority of listeners. The results are in accordance with the findings by Chafe (1980) and Swerts (1998) in that fillers are more frequent at major discourse boundaries than minor ones. Fillers may be functioning as one of the cues to signal topic shifts to listeners.

Figure 4–6 suggests that the patterns of the results differ between the two kinds of presentations, although there was no significant interaction between boundary types and presentation types. While filler rate tends to increase as the boundary strength grows in casual presentations, filler rate at clause boundaries tends to be higher than the rate at sub boundaries and as high as main boundaries in academic presentations. Filler rate at clause boundaries is higher in academic presentations than in casual presentations possibly because clauses tend to be longer in the former than the latter. The results suggest that relationship between boundary depths and filler rates differs depending on the degree of spontaneity of speech. Namely, the more spontaneous the speech, the more closely the filler rates seem to correspond to the boundary strengths. In the next section we focus on the boundary features of casual presentations, which are more spontaneous and more similar to everyday conversations than academic presentations are.

### 4.2.9. Features of syntactic and discourse boundaries in casual presentations

In this section, we more closely examine the features of syntactic and discourse boundaries in casual presentations with discourse segment boundary tags. We measured the durations of silent pauses and filled pauses as well as the rates of fillers and conjunctions at clause and main discourse segment boundaries.

#### 4.2.9.1. Method

Twenty-four casual presentations examined in the previous section were further analyzed. These presentations were given by speakers of Tokyo Japanese, aged between the 20s and the 60s. They were paid volunteers. A half of them were male and another half female speakers. They talked about a general topic such as "the happiest (saddest) experience in my life" or "my town". The topics were given to the speakers previous to the talk. They were instructed to prepare a note for the presentation, and not to read aloud a manuscript. Each presentation lasted between 10 and 15 minutes.

First, we computed the rates of boundaries with filled pauses or with conjunctions for four types of boundaries in each presentation, i.e. *Type B*, *Type C*, *Type D* and main discourse boundaries (we call them *Type E* boundaries, hereafter). We employed only main boundaries as discourse boundaries because many sub boundaries coincide with main boundaries. We compared the mean rates of boundaries with filled pauses or with conjunctions among four boundary types. Second, we measured the durations of silent and filled pauses at four types of boundaries. We took the median of the durations in each category for each presentation, and compared the mean values over presentations among four types of boundaries.

#### 4.2.9.2. Results

Table 4–6 shows the mean number of each boundary type.

Table 4–6 The mean number of each boundary type

| Type | B | C | D | E |
|---|---|---|---|---|
| Mean number | 56 | 62 | 37 | 12 |

Figure 4–7 illustrates the rates of filled pauses and conjunctions at four types of boundaries. The rate of filled pauses increases gradually whereas the rate of conjunctions increases linearly with the boundary strengths. A one-way repeated measures analysis of variance (ANOVA) showed a significant effect of boundary type on the rate of filled pauses, $F(3, 69) = 17.63, p < .001$. Paired comparisons (alpha adjusted by Bonferroni) revealed that the rate of filled pauses at *Type E* boundaries was significantly higher than the rate at any other type of boundaries, B vs. E: $t(23) = 5.48, p < .001$; C vs. E: $t(23) = 3.85, p < .005$; D vs. E: $t(23) = 4.62, p < .001$. The rate of filled pauses at *Type C* boundaries was significantly higher than the rate at *Type B* boundaries, $t(23) = 4.80, p < .001$. There was no significant difference between the rates at *Type D* and *Type B* boundaries, or *Type D* type and *Type C* boundaries, B vs. D: $t(23) = 1.64, p = .69$; C vs. D: $t(23) = 1.94, p = .39$., The rate of filled pauses at clause and discourse boundaries corresponded to the boundary strengths. However, the rate of filled pauses at sentence boundaries was not significantly different from the rates at clause boundaries.

Regarding the rate of conjunctions, a one-way repeated measures ANOVA showed a significant effect of boundary type, $F(3, 69) = 90.49, p < .001$. Paired comparisons (alpha adjusted by Bonferroni) revealed that the stronger the boundary, the higher the rate of conjunctions. The rate at *Type E* boundaries was significantly higher than the rate at any other type of boundaries, B vs. E: $t(23) = 14.18, p < .001$; C vs. E: $t(23) = 11.64, p < .001$; D vs. E: $t(23) = 5.63, p < .001$. The rate at *Type D* boundaries was significantly higher than the rates at *Type C* and *Type B* boundaries, B vs. D: $t(23) = 8.81, p < .001$; C vs. D: $t(23) = 4.98, p < .001$. The rate at *Type C* boundaries was significantly higher than the rate at *Type B* boundaries, $t(23) = 7.37, p < .001$. The rate of conjunctions more clearly corresponded to the boundary strengths than the rate of filled pauses did.

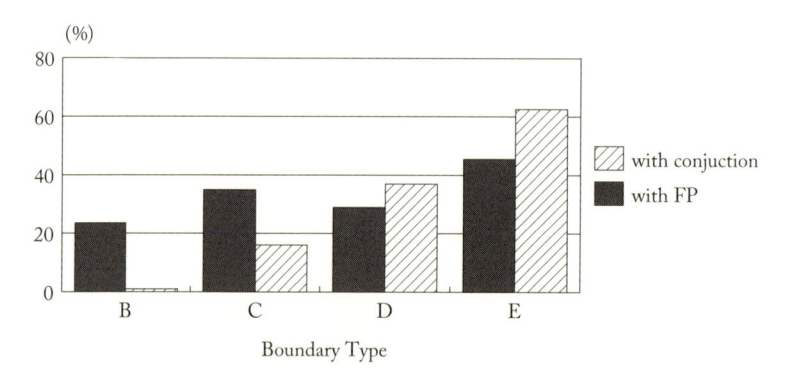

Figure 4–7 The rate of boundaries with filled pauses (FP) and with conjunctions

Figure 4–8 illustrates the durations of silent pauses when there was neither filled pause nor conjunction (the left bar at each boundary type) and when there was a filled pause (the right bar). A two-way repeated measures ANOVA (boundary type × with or without filled pause) showed a main effect of boundary type, $F(3, 42) = 10.44, p < .001$. There was no significant main effect of with or without filled pause condition, $F(1, 14) = 2.47, p = .14$. There was no significant interaction between the two factors either, $F(3, 42) = .940, p = .39$. Paired comparisons (alpha adjusted by Bonferroni) revealed that the silent pause durations at *Type E* boundaries were significantly longer than the durations at any other type of boundaries, B vs. E: $t(14) = 4.21, p < .001$; C vs. E: $t(14) = 3.87, p < .01$; D vs. E: $t(14) = 42.66, p < .05$. The pauses at *Type C* and *Type D* boundaries were significantly longer than the pauses at *Type B* boundaries, B vs. C: $t(14) = 2.17, p < .05$; B vs. D: $t(14) = 2.11, p < .05$. There was no significant difference between the durations at *Type C* and *Type D* boundaries, $t(14) = 1.71, p = .11$.

Similar to the rate of filled pauses, the duration of silent pauses between two consecutive clauses positively corresponded to the boundary strengths of clauses.

However, the pauses at sentence boundaries were not significantly longer than the pauses at *Type C* clause boundaries.

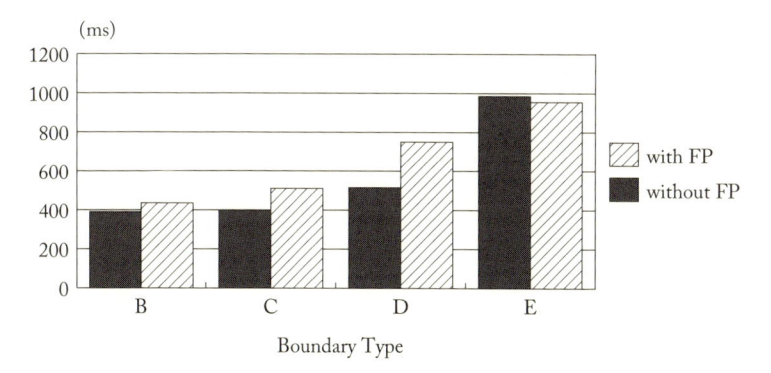

Figure 4–8 The duration of silent pauses with and without filled pauses followed at four types of boundaries

Table 4–7 illustrates the durations of filled pauses (from the onset of filler sounds up to the end of the following silence if any) at four types of boundaries. A one-way repeated measures ANOVA showed a marginal effect of boundary type, $F(3, 57) = 3.96, p = .06$. The filled pauses at *Type E* boundaries tended to be longer than the others.

Table 4–7 The duration of filled pauses at four types of boundaries

| Boundary type | B | C | D | E |
|---|---|---|---|---|
| Filled pause (ms) | 274 | 248 | 278 | 804 |

### 4.2.9.3. Discussion

The rates of filled pauses and conjunctions both corresponded to the boundary strengths. However, the conjunction rates showed clearer correspondence to the boundary strengths than the filler rates.

The duration of silent pauses corresponded to boundary strengths. The stronger the boundary, the longer the silent pauses tended to be. This finding is consistent with the results in Section 4.2.7. However, silent pauses at *Type D* boundaries (sentence boundaries with main discourse boundaries excluded) were not significantly longer than the pauses at *Type C* clause boundaries. It is possible that weak sentence boundaries are not much stronger than *Type C* clause boundaries in terms of the content of speech.

The durations of filled pauses showed no correspondence to boundary strengths except for the case with *Type E* boundaries. Filled pauses at *Type E* boundaries tended to be longer than the others. Once filled pauses are uttered, their durations may be affected by factors other than the boundary strength itself. The degree of planning difficulties of the following parts of speech can be one of the factors.

Research on Dutch filled pauses showed that the F0 values of filled pauses tended to be higher at stronger boundaries than at weaker boundaries, although their durations did not significantly differ between the two boundary types. Differences may be found in F0 values of filled pauses according to boundary strengths in Japanese as well as in Dutch.

## 4.3. Testing the Complexity Hypothesis

In the previous section we tested the boundary hypothesis at clause, sentence, and discourse boundaries. In the present section we test the complexity hypothesis, the more complex the following constituents, the higher the disfluency rate, by first examining filler rates at sentence and clause boundaries. As the findings suggest that filler rate corresponds to complexity of units smaller than clauses, we also test the hypothesis by examining filler rates at phrase boundaries. We take boundary strengths into account in testing the complexity hypothesis, because we know from the results in the previous section that filler rate tends to correspond to boundary strengths.

### 4.3.1. Method

The speech material was the same as that in the previous section. We analysed 177 academic and casual presentations in "the Core" in CSJ. Three presentations were excluded from analysis because the recording staff of the presentation noted that the speaker read the manuscript. Thus, 174 presentations (68 academic and 106 casual) were retained for the present analysis.

Clauses were grouped according to the number of consisting words at four words interval. The rate of clause boundaries containing fillers with or without preceding conjunctions as a function of the number of words in the following clause was calculated by each boundary type for each presentation. Then, the rates were averaged over presentations. The rate of clauses containing fillers not only at the beginning but also in the middle of the clause was also computed. As conjunctions are likely to play a role similar to fillers, particularly at *Type D* boundaries, as was mentioned in the previous section, the rate of clause boundaries with conjunctions with or without preceding or following fillers was also calculated.

### 4.3.2. Results

#### 4.3.2.1. The rate of clause boundaries with fillers

Figure 4–9 shows the rate of each type of clause boundaries with fillers with or without preceding conjunctions as a function of the number of words in the following clause. The rate of boundaries with fillers gradually rises as the number of words in the following clause increases for *Type B* and *Type C* boundaries. However, hardly any increase in the filler rate is observed for *Type D* (sentence) boundaries.

The rates of *Type B* and *Type C* boundaries with fillers (in %) can be approximated well with the following model:

$$y = 0.32x - 13b + 36,$$

where y is a rate of clause boundaries with fillers; x is a maximum number of words in the word group binned at four words; b is whether the boundary type is B (b = 1) or not (b = 0); R = .95, R Square = .90. Standardised coefficients indicate that the boundary type factor has a larger effect on the rate of boundaries with fillers than the length factor, standardised coefficients for b = - 0.82; for x = 0.47.

The clauses were further grouped into three according to the number of words to enable inter-group comparisons: clauses with one to eight words were grouped as short clauses; clauses with nine to 16 words were regarded as medium length clauses (called "medium"), and clauses with more than 16 words were grouped as long clauses. Figure 4–10 describes the rates of three types of boundaries with fillers before short (1–8 words), medium (9–16) and long (17-) clauses.

Two-way repeated measures analysis of variance (ANOVA) with boundary type as one factor and with length of the following clause with the other showed main effects of the boundary type factor $F(2, 340) = 63.93$, $p < .001$, and the length factor, $F(2, 340) = 12.12$, $p < .001$. An interaction between the two factors was significant, $F(4, 680) = 4.02$, $p < .005$.

We first compared the rates by boundary type. As for *Type B* boundaries, there was a significant difference among length conditions, $F(2, 169) = 14.39$, $p < .001$. Paired comparisons (adjusted by Bonferroni) revealed that the rate of fillers before long clauses was significantly higher than the rates before short and medium clauses and that the rate of fillers before medium clauses was significantly higher than the rate before short clauses, long vs. short: $t(170) = 5.18$. $p < .001$; long vs. medium: $t(170) = 2.95$, $p < .05$; medium vs. short: $t(170)

= 3.08, $p$ < .007. Namely, the longer the following clause, the higher the rate of the boundaries with fillers, supporting the complexity hypothesis. Regarding *Type C* boundaries, there was a significant difference among length conditions, $F(2, 169) = 4.08$, $p$ < .05. Paired comparisons (adjusted by Bonferroni) revealed that the rate of fillers before long clauses was significantly higher than the rate before short clauses, $t(170) = 2.75$, $p$ < .05. However, there was no significant difference in the rates either between long and medium clauses or between short and medium clauses, long vs. medium: $t(170) = 2.23$, $p = .08$; medium vs. short: $t(170) = 1.00$, $p = .96$. As for *Type D* (sentence) boundaries, there was no significant difference among length conditions, $F(2, 169) = .25$, $p = .78$. Again, as with the boundary hypothesis, the complexity hypothesis was supported by the results with *Type B* and *Type C* clause boundaries, but not with *Type D* (sentence) boundaries.

When we compared the rate by length group, there were significant differences among boundary type conditions in all the length groups, short: $F(2, 169)$

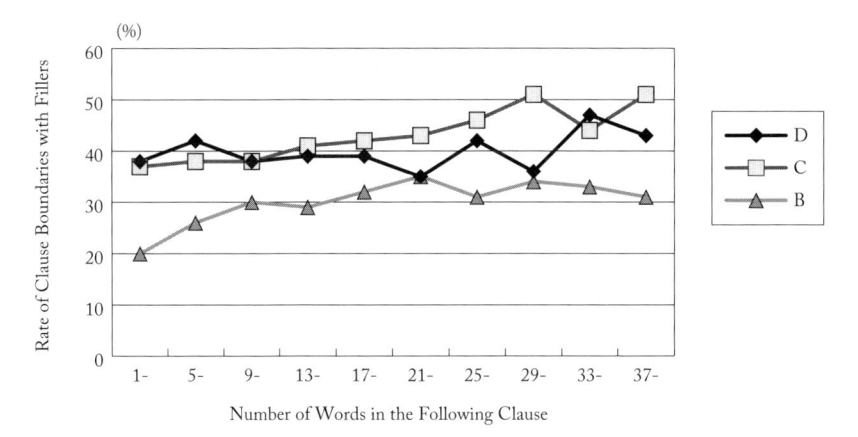

Figure 4–9  The rate of three types of clause boundaries with fillers as a function of the number of words in the following clause

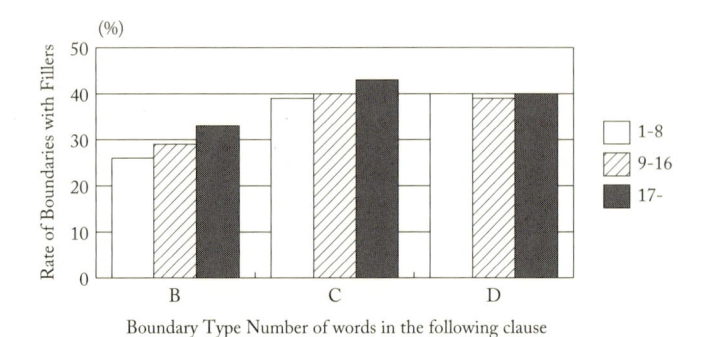

Figure 4–10  Rate of clause boundaries with fillers before short (1–8 words), medium (9–16 words) and long (17– words) clauses

= 66.66, $p$ < .001; medium: $F$ (2, 169) = 50.64, $p$ < .001; long: $F$ (2, 169) = 15.02, $p$ < .001. Paired comparisons (adjusted by Bonferroni) showed that in all the length groups, the rates of fillers at *Type C* and *Type D* boundaries were significantly higher than those at *Type B* boundaries, but that there were no significant differences between the rates at *Type C* and *Type D* boundaries. The results are summarised in Table 4–8. Regardless of the length of the following clause, filler rates at *Type C* and *Type D* boundaries were significantly higher than the rate at *Type B* boundaries, and there was no significant difference between *Type C* and *Type D* boundaries.

#### 4.3.2.2. The rate of clauses with fillers

Figure 4–11 illustrates the rate of clauses with fillers at the beginning (i.e. at the preceding clause boundary) or in the middle of clauses. The rate of clauses containing fillers increased roughly linearly as the number of words in the clause grew with similar slopes after all the boundary types. The rates of clauses containing fillers are almost identical after *Type C* and *Type D* boundaries. The rates of clauses with fillers after three types of boundaries (in %) can be well approximated with the following linear model obtained through a multiple regression analysis:

$$y = 1.45x - 10.35b + 36.9,$$

where y is a rate of clauses with fillers; x is a maximum number of words in the word group binned at four words; b is whether the boundary type is B (b = 1) or not (b = 0), R = .97, R Square = .94. The standardised coefficients indicate that the length of clauses have a dominant effect on the rates of clauses containing fillers anywhere in the clause, standardised coefficients for x = 0.93; for b = - 0.27.

The rate of clauses with fillers can be approximated without taking clause boundary types into account fairly well with the following linear model:

$$y = 1.45x + 33.5,$$

where y is a rate of clauses with fillers; x is a maximum number of words in the word group binned at four words, R = .93, R Square = .87.

These results, together with the results mentioned in Section 4.3.2.1 indicate that fillers appear not necessarily at the beginning but somewhere in the

Table 4–8 Results of pair-wise comparisons by length group

| Clause length | Boundary type | df | t | sig. |
|---|---|---|---|---|
| short | B vs. C | 170 | 8.75* | $p < .001$ |
|  | B vs. D | 170 | 9.85* | $p < .001$ |
|  | C vs. D | 170 | .80 | $p = 1.00$ |
| medium | B vs. C | 170 | 9.78* | $p < .001$ |
|  | B vs. D | 170 | 6.76* | $p < .001$ |
|  | C vs. D | 170 | .62 | $p = 1.00$ |
| long | B vs. C | 170 | 5.44* | $p < .001$ |
|  | B vs. D | 170 | 3.45* | $p < .002$ |
|  | C vs. D | 170 | 1.85 | $p = .20$ |

*The mean difference is significant at the .05 level.
Adjustment for multiple comparisons: Bonferroni.

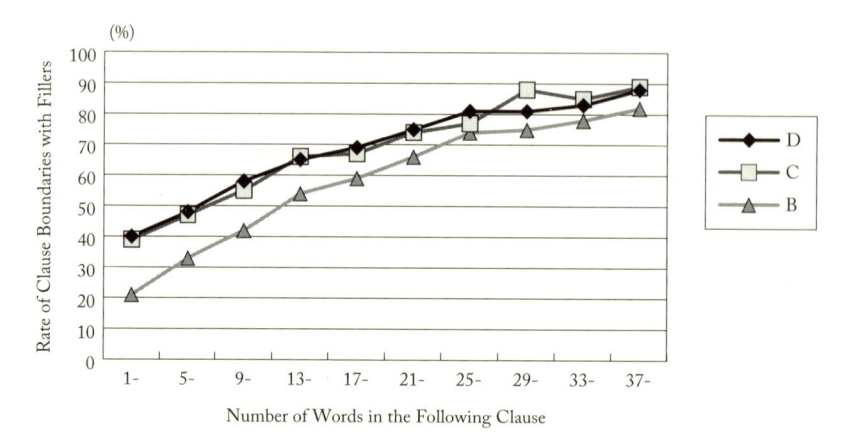

Figure 4–11  Rate of clauses with fillers after 3 types of boundaries as a function of the number of words in the clause

clause when the clause becomes longer. Longer clauses are likely to contain other clauses (adjective or noun clauses). It is possible that fillers appear at other types of clause boundaries in adverbial clauses. Another possibility is that fillers appear at boundaries of constituents smaller than clauses or within a constituent. In any case, the results suggest that fillers tend to correspond to units smaller than adverbial clauses.

#### 4.3.2.3. The rate of clauses with conjunctions

Figure 4–12 illustrates the rate of each type of clause boundaries with conjunctions as a function of the number of words in the following clause. The rate of *Type D* boundaries with conjunctions increases up to the third words group (9 to 12 words) and stays almost constant after that point. This would mean that the rate of conjunctions at sentence boundaries has some correspondence with the length of the following clause when the clause contains less than nine words. However, the rates of conjunctions at *Type B* and *Type C* boundaries are constant

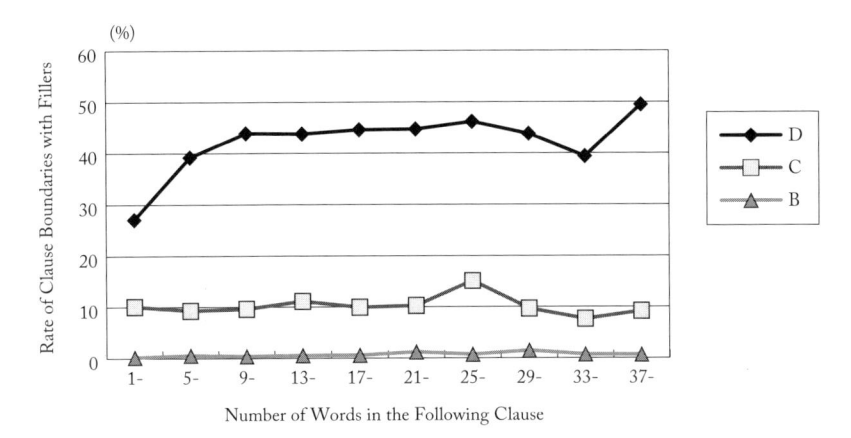

Figure 4–12  Rate of three types of clause boundaries with conjunctions as a function of the number of words in the following clause

regardless of number of words in the following clause. The results indicate that the length of the following clause does not affect the rate of conjunctions at clause boundaries except for *Type D* (sentence) boundaries followed by clauses with less than nine words. The results suggest that fillers and conjunctions are triggered by different factors at sentence and clause boundaries.

### 4.3.3. Discussion

The complexity hypothesis was most clearly supported by the filler rate at *Type B* boundaries, weakly supported by the rate at *Type C* boundaries, and not supported by the rate at sentence boundaries. It is assumed that the deeper the boundary, the more conceptual planning speakers are required. The finding that the effects of complexity of the following clause are stronger at shallower boundaries indicates that complexity of the following constituents has effects on filler rate only when less conceptualisation takes place. The results suggest that speakers plan certain limited number of constituents when they are mainly engaged in conceptualisation.

The rate of clauses containing fillers somewhere in the clause increased roughly linearly as the number of words in the clause grew, regardless of boundary types. This finding indicates that filler rate corresponds to the number of words in the following constituents, but that the corresponding unit is smaller than a clause.

Unlike the rate of clause boundaries with fillers, the rate of clause boundaries with conjunctions hardly corresponded to the number of words in the following clause. This finding suggests that conjunctions are uttered by mechanisms different from those of fillers, although conjunctions seem to play a role as time gaining device for speakers as fillers do, particularly at sentence boundaries.

In the next section, we examine filler rates at bunsetu phrase boundaries within clauses to test the complexity hypothesis, because the results suggest that filler rate corresponds to units smaller than clauses. Bunsetu comprises one content word with or without function words, which often composes an accentual phrase in Japanese.

### 4.3.4. Filler rate at bunsetu phrase boundaries

#### 4.3.4.1. Method

The speech material was the same as the previous section: We analysed 174 presentations (68 academic and 106 casual) in the Core in CSJ. The heads of modifying bunsetu phrases are tagged in the transcripts of presentations in the Core. We used these tags. We regarded the number of bunsetu phrases between modifying and modified bunsetu phrases as an index to the complexity of the constituents following the modifying phrase. We gave the value "one" when a phrase modified the following phrase, "two" when a phrase modified the one after the next phrase, and so forth. We examined filler rates immediately after modifying bunsetu phrases as a function of the number of bunsetu phrases up to the modified phrase in each presentation, and averaged them over presentations.

### 4.3.4.2. Results and discussion

Figure 4–13 illustrates the mean filler rate of those immediately after modifying bunsetu phrases as a function of the number of bunsetu phrases up to the modified phrase. The numbers on the x-axis indicate the numbers of bunsetu phrases between the modifying and modified phrases. The rightmost bar shows the rate of cases in which there were more than six phrases between modifying and modified phrases.

Figure 4–13 demonstrates that the filler rate increases roughly linearly as a function of number of bunsetu phrases between the modifier and the head, except when phrases modify the following phrase, in which case filler rate is extremely low (1%). This finding supports the complexity hypothesis, and indicates frequent locations of fillers within clauses. The filler rates after modifying bunsetu phrase boundaries are approximately as high as the rates after clause boundaries, suggesting that a bunsetu phrase is another important unit of planning in Japanese.

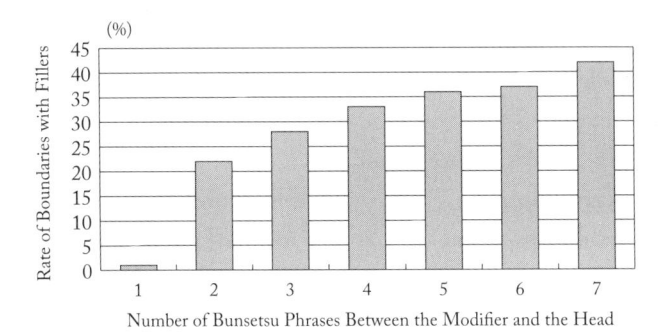

Figure 4–13 Rate of phrase boundaries with fillers as a function of number of bunsetu phrases between the modifier and the head

## 4.4. Chapter Summary

In this chapter we tested two hypotheses about factors affecting filler rates at phrase, clause, sentence and discourse boundaries, the boundary hypothesis and the complexity hypothesis.

In Section 4.2, we tested the boundary hypothesis which presumes that the deeper the boundary the higher the disfluency rate, by examining filler rates at clause, sentence, and discourse boundaries in presentations. The boundary hypothesis was supported by filler rates at clause boundaries of different strengths, but filler rate at sentence boundaries, which is assumed to be stronger than clause boundaries, was not higher than the rate at *Type C* clause boundaries. We considered two possibilities to explain the results: 1) Speakers may employ different strategies such as using the time while uttering conjunctions to plan the contents of the following speech at sentence boundaries; 2) There is hardly any difference in strengths of boundaries between *Type C* boundaries and sentence boundaries in spontaneous speech. We found that the rate of conjunctions was higher and silent pause duration was longer at sentence boundaries than at *Type C* clause boundaries. We also reported that silent pauses were longer when they were followed by fillers than when they were not at any type of boundaries. These findings indicate that sentence boundaries are stronger boundaries than clause boundaries in spontaneous speech as well as in written texts, and that filler rate at sentence boundaries was not higher than at *Type C* clause boundaries because speakers can make use of the time of uttering conjunctions and longer silent pauses as well as filled pauses to plan the contents of the following utterance.

Filler rate at discourse boundaries at which majority of listeners recognised a topic shift was higher than the rate at sentence or *Type C* clause boundaries in casual presentations. This finding supported the boundary hypothesis and is in accordance with the results of Dutch filled pauses. However, the hypothesis was not supported by filler rates in academic presentations: The filler rate at sentence boundaries and *Type C* clause boundaries was as high as the rate at main discourse boundaries. These findings suggest that occurrence of filled pauses is affected by speech genres and/or degree of spontaneity as well as boundary strength.

In Section 4.3, by examining filler rates at sentence, clause, and bunsetu phrase boundaries, we tested the complexity hypothesis that the more complex the following constituents, the higher the disfluency rate. The complexity hypothesis was supported by the filler rates at phrase and clause boundaries, but not by the rate at sentence boundaries. The effects of boundary strength were larger than the effects of complexity of the following constituents at sentence and clause boundaries. The effects of complexity tended to be more obvious at weaker boundaries, or boundaries of smaller units, among the boundary types examined.

These results indicate that complexity of the following constituent is relevant to filler rates at boundaries only in case in which less conceptual planning is required. As conceptual planning requires attention, speakers seem to be able to plan only a limited number of constituents when they are occupied with conceptualising a message at deeper boundaries.

# Chapter 5

# Effects of Filled Pauses on Listeners' Expectation about the Upcoming Speech

## 5.1. Chapter Overview

In this chapter, we examine whether filled pauses affect listeners' predictions about the complexity of upcoming phrases. As was mentioned in Chapter 2, studies of spontaneous speech corpora show that constituents tend to be longer or more complex when they are immediately preceded by filled pauses than when they are not. From this finding, we hypothesized that filled pauses cause listeners to expect that the speaker is going to refer to something that is likely to be expressed by a relatively long or complex constituent. We discuss the hypothesis more in detail in Section 5.2.

In the experiments, described in Section 5.3 and Section 5.4, participants listened to sentences describing both simple and compound shapes on a computer screen. Their task was to press a button as soon as they had identified the shape corresponding to the description. Phrases describing shapes were immediately preceded by a filled pause, a silent pause of the same duration, or no pause. We predicted that listeners' response times to compound shapes would be shorter when there is a filled pause before phrases describing the shape than when there is no filled pause, because filled pauses are good cues to complex phrases, whereas response times to simple shapes would not be shorter with a preceding filled pause than without. The results of native Japanese and proficient non-native Chinese listeners agreed with the prediction and provided evidence to support the hypothesis. However, response times of the least proficient non-native listeners were not affected by the existence of filled pauses. The results with Chinese speakers suggest that the effects of filled pauses on non-native listeners depend on their language proficiency. Section 5.5 summarises the chapter.

## 5.2. Introduction

As mentioned in Section 2.4.2, disfluencies are more frequent before relatively long or complex constituents. This is likely to be because long or complex constituents are more difficult to formulate and take speakers longer to plan than short or simple constituents. In conversations, one alternates between one's roles as a speaker and a listener. Therefore, it is plausible to assume that what one experiences as a speaker affects one's behaviour as a listener. It is also possible that listeners are utilizing filled pauses as probabilistic cues to the onset of relatively large constituents, as Bailey and Ferreira (2003) argued. We hypothesized from the findings of corpus-based studies that listeners expect a relatively long or complex phrase to follow when there is a filled pause. In other words, we predicted that filled pauses cause listeners to expect that the speaker is going to refer to something that requires a relatively long or complex constituent to express. Although the length measured by the number of words in a constituent and its syntactic complexity are not logically connected, they are highly correlated (Wasow, 2002). Therefore, we did not distinguish these two factors in this study. We have chosen to examine the effects of filled pauses on listeners because filled pauses are far more common than any other type of disfluencies in Japanese (Maekawa, 2004).

We composed utterances in which either a simple or a complex phrase appeared to refer to an object. Some of the phrases were preceded by a filled pause, and others had no preceding filled pauses. We predicted that listeners would be able to process a complex phrase more quickly when there is a filled pause before the phrase than when there is no filled pause. We assumed that filled pauses give a cue to the speaker's planning difficulty and allow listeners some time to predict the content of the upcoming speech. Consequently, listeners will be able to respond to the referent of a complex phrase more quickly with a preceding filled pause than without. On the other hand, as filled pauses are not so frequent before simple phrases as before complex phrases, filled pauses before simple phrases are not likely to help listeners' predictions. As a result, responses to the referent of a simple phrase will not be quicker, or could even be slower with a preceding filled pause than without.

We conducted experiments with Chinese speakers of Japanese as well as with native Japanese speakers to test the hypothesis. We assumed that it is a universal linguistic tendency that filled pauses are more frequent before longer or more complex constituents. However, as disfluencies have language specific aspects in terms of sounds and forms, listeners would probably need to be exposed to spontaneous speech of a non-native language long enough to be able to recognize and process disfluencies in a non-native language effectively. In Japanese, for example, one of the most frequent fillers, *ano* has a function as a demonstrative adjective similar to *that* in English as well as that of a filler. If non-native Japanese speakers only know *ano* as a demonstrative adjective, they may have trouble in processing *ano* as a filler.

It has widely been observed that the effects of experimental conditions depend on the learners' proficiency levels in the language (e.g. Chiang & Dunkel, 1992, Rubin, 1994). Therefore, non-native participants were grouped into three groups according to their proficiency levels in spoken Japanese. The results were compared among the three groups as well as with the results of native Japanese listeners. It was not known what effect filled pauses at phrase boundaries have on non-native listeners because there has hardly been any research directly related to this topic. However, we predicted that the higher their proficiency in spoken Japanese, the more similar their response pattern to that of the native listeners.

## 5.3. Experiment 1 with Native Listeners

### 5.3.1. Participants

Thirty university students who are native speakers of Tokyo (standard) Japanese took part in the experiment. They were paid 700 Yen each.

### 5.3.2. Design

A pair of shapes of the same colour were presented on a computer screen, where one consisted of a simple shape (circle, triangle or square) and the other a compound shape (two arrows attached to a paired shape. See Fig. 5–1). One second after the appearance of the visual stimulus, speech referring to one of the two shapes was played. The participants' task was to press a button corresponding to the shape being referred to as soon as possible. The instructions given to the participants were as follows (translated from Japanese): "A woman is asking her interlocutor to bring a paper decoration in a certain colour and a shape. Which one is she asking for? Two pieces of paper appear on the computer screen. Please press either the left or right mouse button corresponding to the piece of paper that she is asking for as soon as possible." Through these instructions, we aimed at making the participants guess what would follow the filled pauses. In everyday life, it is not uncommon to infer what the speaker is going to say next when the speaker pauses or hesitates, especially when one is interested in the talk or when one wants to be cooperative with the speaker. We assumed that the participants would do what they normally do even in an experimental setting, although the

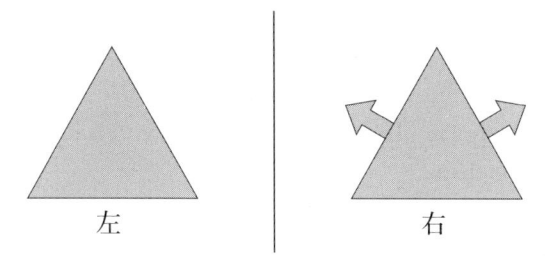

5    Effects of Filled Pauses on Listeners' Expectation about the Upcoming Speech    103

左                    右

Figure 5–1   An example of visual stimuli: The visual stimuli always consisted of a simple shape (round, square or triangular) and a compound shape (with two arrows attached to the simple shape). The two shapes were always displayed in the same colour. Kanji (Chinese) characters were allocated under the figures, indicating "left" for the left figure and "right" for the right figure.

utterances of this experiment are not ones that would typically be heard repeatedly in everyday life. The answer choices were limited to two in the experiment, and this may seem unnatural at a glance. However, it is not unusual in everyday life that the possible following types of utterances are limited by the situational or linguistic contexts and highly predictable for the listener. For example, if a family member says at the breakfast table, "Can you pass me the …," the possible word following "the" will be a noun or an adjective and the referent of the noun phrase will be limited to one of the items on the table or in the space which the speaker is looking at. The types of utterances in the second parts of adjacency pairs, such as answers to yes-no questions, responses to requests or invitations, are also highly predictable.

Each utterance contained a phrase describing a colour (called "a colour phrase") and a phrase describing a shape ("a shape phrase") in this order. As paired shapes were always in the same colour, the colour phrases were not relevant to the task. The target phrases were shape phrases.

The experiment involved two factors:
1) **Complexity factor**: the speech stimuli referred to either a simple shape or a

compound shape ("simple condition" and "complex condition," respectively). We assumed one is aware that more words or a complex structure is usually necessary to describe compound shapes than simple shapes, and therefore, it takes one longer to plan constituents referring to compound shapes than those of simple shapes.

2) **Fluency factor**: Target phrases (i.e. shape phrases) were immediately preceded by the filled pause *eto* pronounced most frequently /ɛːto/ (the vowels and the consonant of which can be shorter or longer), a silent pause of the same duration as a filled pause, or no pause ("filler condition," "pause condition," and "fluent condition," respectively).

Example sentences in simple and complex conditions with filled pauses are given below with English translations. Fillers are in italics. The sentences are shown separated into bunsetu phrases by spaces. Bunsetu phrases are linguistic units comprising one content word with or without function words. One or more bunsetu phrases compose a prosodic phrase in fluent speech.

(1) Simple condition with a filled pause:
Ano-ne, watasi-no heya-kara akaku-te *eto* marui kami mottekite-kureru ?
Dem-Par I-Gen room-Abl red-Con *um* circular paper bring-Aux
Look, could you bring red and *um* circular paper from my room?

(2) Complex condition with a filled pause:
Ano-ne, watasi-no heya-kara akaku-te *eto* maru-ni yajirusi-ga tui-ta kami mottekite-kureru ?
Dem-Par I-Gen room-Abl red-Con *um* circle-Dat arrow-Nom attach-Aux paper bring-Aux
Look, could you bring red and *um* circular paper with arrows from my room?

(Abl: ablative; Aux: auxiliary; Con: connective, Dat: dative; Dem: demonstrative; Gen: genitive; Nom: nominative; Par: particle)

In the simple condition, shape phrases were composed of one bunsetu phrase with one or two words. In the complex condition, shape phrases consisted of three bunsetu phrases, each of which contained two words. Shape phrases in the complex condition were both longer and more complex than those in the simple condition.

The filler *eto* was used because it is one of the most frequent types of fillers both in dialogues and monologues. This sound form exclusively functions as a filler, while most other types have functions other than fillers. Another reason was that *eto* was chosen by eight out of ten native speakers of Japanese who were asked to choose one filler they would use in this context among the four frequent types, *ano*, *e*, *eto*, and *ma*. All of the informants reported that *ano* and *e* could also be used in this context, but not *ma*. Functions of *eto*, *ano*, and *e*, in this context, therefore, seem very similar, and it is likely that findings of the experiments with *eto* can be generalised to *ano* and *e*.

The silent pause condition was added for the following reasons. When the results in the filler condition differed from those in the fluent condition, we would not know whether the difference was attributable to the time that filled pauses allowed listeners or both the time and the sound of them. Comparison of the effects of filled pauses with those of silent pauses of the same duration would reveal whether the effects are derived from the time or both the time and the sound of filled pauses. If the results of the filler condition differed from those of the pause condition, the difference would be attributable to the sounds of fillers. If not, it is likely that the effects of filled pauses mainly resulted from the time they took rather than their sounds.

### 5.3.3. Auditory and visual stimuli

Speech stimuli were created in the following way. The author uttered sentences with a structure as follows:

| Ano-ne | $1-kara | $2 te | eto | $3 | kami | mottekite-kureru? |
|--------|---------|-------|-----|-----|------|-------------------|
| Dem-Par | place-Abl | colour-and | um | shape | paper | bring-Aux |

Each slot was filled with one of the words or phrases in Japanese below:

$1: on the desk, my room, next room

$2: black, blue, brown, green, grey, orange, pink, purple, red, yellow

$3: circular, circle with arrows, square, square with arrows, triangular, triangle with arrows

Thus, 180 sentences were created.

$1 (3 items) × $2 (10 items) × $3 (6 items) = 180

Although the test stimuli were presented to the speaker as a reading list, the speaker uttered the sentences without looking at the list so that the utterances sounded like natural, everyday speech. The utterances were recorded in an acoustically treated recording studio. The speech was sampled at 44 kHz and digitised at 16 bits directly onto a PC.

All the utterances contained the filler *eto* between the colour word and the shape word. *eto* was always preceded by a short silent pause, which accords with the tendency that the majority of *eto* are preceded by a silent pause (Watanabe & Ishii, 2000). Some *eto* were immediately followed by shape words, while others were followed by short silent pauses. The onsets of shape words were one of the following consonants, /m/ for *maru* (circle); /s/ for *sankaku* (triangle); /ɕ/ (voiceless alveolo-palatal median laminal fricative) for *shikaku* (square).

We called the original speech *a filler version*. The original speech was digitally edited and two new versions were created. Figure 5–2 shows the editing process of the original speech.

1) *A pause version*: filled pauses were substituted by silence of the same duration as the filled pauses.

2) *A fluent version*: filled pauses (i.e. *eto* with short, adjacent silence) were edited out.

Short silence before and after *eto* enabled us to modify speech without making editing noise or creating unnatural F0 contours.

Speech stimuli were checked by two native speakers of Japanese. They reported no unnaturalness about the speech. Table 1 shows the mean duration of speech stimuli in each condition and the mean durations of silent and filled pauses in simple and complex conditions. In the fluent condition, sentences with complex target phrases were 993ms longer than sentences with simple target phrases (4912ms vs. 3919ms), as the former contained eight moras more than the latter. Filled pauses in the complex condition were 224ms longer than those in the simple condition (953ms vs. 729ms).

Three sets of stimuli (A, B, C), each of which contained 180 sentences, were created so that only one of the three versions of the same utterances appeared in each stimuli set. All the speech stimuli in set A were checked by a native speaker of Japanese, who reported no unnaturalness about the speech. The mean duration of speech stimuli in each condition is given in Table 5–1. The amplitude of speech stimuli was normalised.

Visual stimuli were created so that the half of the correct answers were assigned to the left mouse button and the other half to the right mouse button in each condition in each stimuli set. The experiment was set up using SuperLab Pro.

### 5.3.4. Procedure

The experiment was individually carried out in quiet rooms at Chiba University and the University of Tokyo, in Japan. Participants were randomly assigned to one of the three stimuli sets. After eight practice trials, the participants listened to 180 sentences. The order of stimuli was randomised for each participant. Speech stimuli were presented through stereo headphones. Sentences were played to the end regardless of when the participants pressed the response button. Time out was set at about 300 ms after the end of sentences. When participants pressed

## Filler (Original) Version

| k | iː | r | o | k | t | e | sp | e | t | o | s | a | N | ka | k | n | i | a | dʒ | i | sh | g | a |

[Hz]
300
200
100

$\underbrace{\qquad\qquad\qquad\qquad}$
filled pause, *eto*

## Pause Version

[Hz]
300
200
100

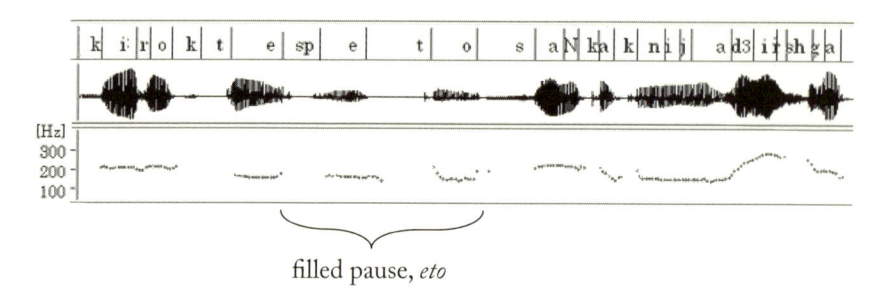

## Fluent Version

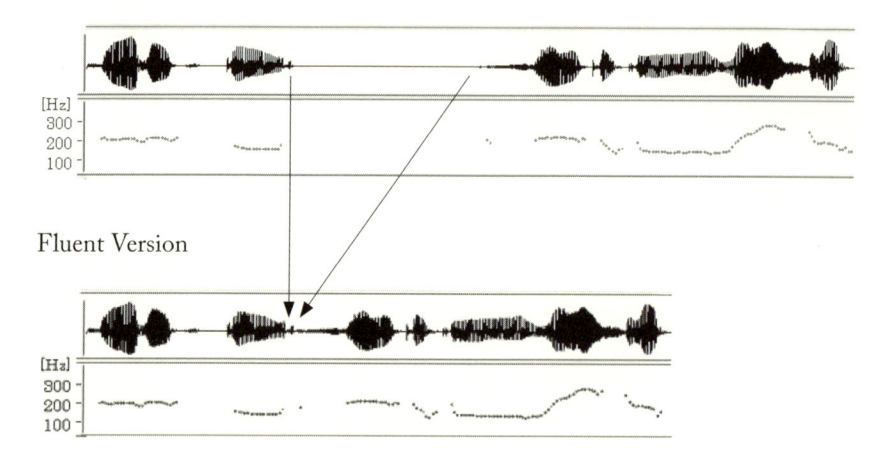

[Hz]
300
200
100

Figure 5–2  An example of editing of speech stimuli, with their transcriptions, speech waves, and F0 contours. *sp* in the transcription stands for silent pause. The filler (original) version contained *eto* between "kiirokute" (yellow and) and "sankaku" (triangle). The pause version was created by substituting *eto* with silence of the same duration. The fluent version was produced by editing out *eto* with the adjacent pauses (a preceding pause in this sample) from the filler version.

a button more than once, only the first answer was taken. There were three second intervals between the trials. The experiment lasted 35 minutes excluding the practice session and a short break in the middle.

After having finished 180 trials, all the participants were asked whether they found anything unnatural in the speech they heard. None of the participants reported any unnaturalness.

Response times from the beginning of the sound files were automatically measured. The onset of the first words describing a shape was manually marked referring to speech sound, sound waves and sound spectrograms. In the example sentences (1) and (2), the word onsets were marked at the beginning of /s/ in *sankaku* (triangle). Response times from the word onset were calculated by subtracting the word onset time from response times measured from the beginning of sound files. The median of the correct response times in each condition for each participant was taken, and the mean median times across conditions were compared.

Table 5–1 Mean duration of speech stimuli in each condition and mean durations of filled pauses in simple and complex conditions

| Conditions | Mean durations (ms) |
| --- | --- |
| Simple | |
| Fluent | 3,919 |
| Filler / Pause | 4,648 |
| (Filled pauses) | 729 |
| Complex | |
| Fluent | 4,912 |
| Filler / Pause | 5,865 |
| (Filled pauses) | 935 |

### 5.3.5. Results

One sentence was excluded from analysis because of a defect of the experiment. Three sentences, the error rates of which exceeded 20 % in one of the stimuli sets, were also excluded from analysis. The mean correct response rate of the remaining trials was 98.3%. The rate of correct responses in each condition is given in Table 5–2. Error responses were excluded from the subsequent analysis.

The mean response times in six conditions are shown in Fig. 5–3. A two-way repeated measures analysis of variance (ANOVA) revealed a main effect of the complexity factor, $F(1, 29) = 74.66, p < .001$, but no main effect of the fluency factor, $F(2,58) = 1.40, p = .25$. A complexity-fluency interaction was significant, $F(2, 58) = 5.85, p < .005$. Post-hoc tests showed a significant difference among fluent conditions in the complex condition, $F(2, 28) = 6.31, p < .005$, but no significant difference in the simple condition, $F(2, 28) = 1.20, p = .32$. Paired comparisons (alpha adjusted by Bonferroni) revealed that response times to complex phrases in the filler condition and in the pause condition were significantly shorter than those in the fluent condition, $t(29) = 3.13, p < .012; t(29) = 3.16, p < .011$, respectively. There was no significant differences between filler-pause conditions, $t(29) = 0.49, p = 1.00$.

Table 5–2  Correct response rate of Japanese participants in each condition

| Conditions | Rates of correct responses (%) |
|---|---|
| Simple | |
| Fluent | 98.1 |
| Filler | 98.9 |
| Pause | 98.9 |
| Complex | |
| Fluent | 97.6 |
| Filler | 99.2 |
| Pause | 97.0 |

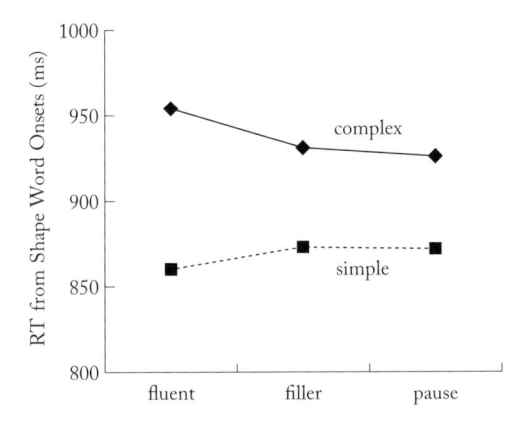

[Figure: plot showing RT from Shape Word Onsets (ms) on y-axis (800–1000) versus fluent, filler, pause conditions on x-axis, with two lines labeled "complex" (around 950 decreasing to ~925) and "simple" (around 860 increasing slightly to ~875).]

Figure 5–3 Japanese participants' mean response times to simple and complex phrases from the onsets of the words describing shapes in the fluent, filler, and pause conditions.

Two-way analyses of variance (ANOVA) over items in three stimuli sets (A, B, C) all showed main effects of the complexity factor, A: $F(1, 170) = 36.46$, $p < .001$; B: $F(1, 170) = 17.74$, $p < .001$; C: $F(1, 170) = 52.71$, $p < .001$, but no main effects of the fluency factor, A: $F(2, 170) = .26$, $p = .77$; B: $F(2, 170) = .81$, $p = .45$; C: $F(2, 170) = 1.71$, $p = .18$. A complexity-fluency interaction was not significant in any of the stimuli sets, A: $F(2, 170) = .65$, $p = .53$; B: $F(2, 170) = .53$, $p = .59$; C: $F(2, 170) = .50$, $p = .61$.

### 5.3.6. Discussion

Response times to complex phrases were shorter when the phrases were immediately preceded by a filled pause than when there was no filled pause. On the other hand, there was no significant difference in response times to simple phrases between fluent-filler conditions. These results showed that the existence of filled pauses accelerated listeners' responses to complex phrases but did not affect their responses to simple phrases. These findings agree with our prediction that filled pauses bias listeners' expectations towards complex phrases.

There was no significant difference in response times between filler-pause conditions in the complex condition. This result suggests that the time that passes during filled pauses is critical for the listeners to be aware of the speaker's planning difficulty and infer the type of upcoming speech. Although no difference was found between the effects of filled and silent pauses, there is a need to further examine whether silent and filled pauses have the same effects in other syntactic contexts. Speakers pause at deep syntactic boundaries such as sentence and clause boundaries at high probabilities, both in read speech and spontaneous speech. Pauses in such locations are assumed to indicate syntactic boundaries and help listeners with speech processing (Sugitou, 1990). Therefore, silent pauses in such locations are unlikely to be perceived as disfluencies even if parts of the pauses are used for speech planning, unless they are extremely long. Consequently, the effects of silent pauses at such locations on listeners may differ from those of filled pauses, as filled pauses more explicitly express speakers' planning difficulties than silent pauses (Fox Tree, 2002).

One may argue that the responses were quicker after filled pauses not because filled pauses biased the listeners' expectations toward complex phrases but because they allowed the listeners extra time for processing the foregoing speech and got them better prepared for the following speech. However, this is not likely. Firstly, responses to simple phrases as well as complex phrases should have been faster after filled pauses if this had been the case. Response times to simple phrases were not shorter after filled pauses than those without pauses, despite the fact that the phrases up to the shape words had the same semantic contents in simple and complex conditions. Secondly, it is unlikely that the listeners needed a pause to process colour words because a pair of shapes in the same colour had been on the computer screen when they heard the colour word, and the colour was known to them before hearing the end of the colour words. In the case of *akaku te* (red and), for example, *ku* is an inflexional suffix and the colour is known to the listeners by the end of *aka*. Therefore, it must have been easy enough for the native listeners to process the colour words without using the following pause.

The results were in line with those of Arnold, Fagnano, and Tanenhaus (2003) and Bailey and Ferreira (2003) in that filled pauses affect the early stage of core language processing of listeners and that they tend to bias listeners' expectations about the upcoming speech towards directions which agree with distributional tendencies of filled pauses and the following constituents. The listeners in Arnold, Fagnano, and Tanenhaus's study tended to expect a discourse-new object rather than discourse-given items, and the participants in Bailey and Ferreira's study as well as those in our study predicted longer constituents after filled pauses. More generally, the results of these studies suggest that listeners are sensitive to speakers' planning difficulties signaled by filled pauses and that filled pauses tend to bias listeners' expectations about upcoming speech towards linguistic expressions which are relatively difficult to access or formulate.

In the next section we test the same hypothesis that listeners tend to expect a relatively long and complex phrase when there is a filled pause with Chinese speakers of Japanese.

## 5.4. Experiment 2 with Non-Native Listeners

### 5.4.1. Participants

44 native speakers of Chinese who had been staying in Japan for more than half a year and have a fairly good command of everyday Japanese took part in the experiment in exchange for 700 Yen. All the participants were either students or researchers at Chiba University or the University of Tokyo, in Japan. As no records of the participants' proficiency levels in Japanese were available, we employed the length of stay in Japan as an index of their proficiency in comprehension of spoken Japanese. We recruited participants so that one third would be those

staying in Japan for the periods of 0.5 - 1.5 years (novice group), another one third for 1.5 - 2.5 years (intermediate group), and the other one third longer than 2.5 years (expert group). We did not include Chinese speakers staying in Japan for less than half a year because their ability of comprehending spoken Japanese could be too divergent to be classified in one group. We also intended to avoid recruiting participants whose listening proficiency was not high enough for the task. The time interval of length of stay for grouping participants was based on our observation that international students using Japanese in their everyday lives make great strides in oral proficiency in the first year after arrival and hardly have any problem carrying on everyday conversation approximately in the third year.

Three participants were excluded from analysis because they turned out to be bilingual speakers of Chinese and other languages. We also excluded participants from analysis if the number of error trials, including trials which timed out, exceeded 10% of the presented trials, to avoid too many missing values. They were substituted with newly recruited participants who belonged to the same proficiency groups. Five participants were substituted for this reason. Thus, data from 36 participants, 12 in each proficiency group, were analysed.

### 5.4.2. Design
The design was the same as Experiment 1 except that the factor of listeners' proficiency in Japanese was added to the analysis. The proficiency factor had three conditions according to the participants' length of stay in Japan: "novice" (0.5–1.5 years), "intermediate" (1.5–2.5 years), and "expert" (longer than 2.5 years).

### 5.4.3. Procedure
The procedure of the experiment was basically the same as that of Experiment 1. However, some participants waited to press the response button until the utterance came to the end in the practice session. In each of these cases the participants were instructed not to wait until the speech ended, but to press the button

as soon as they knew the answer. They did four additional practice trials before starting the experiment.

After having finished 180 trials, all the participants were asked whether they found anything unnatural in the speech which they heard. None of the participants reported any unnaturalness.

### 5.4.4. Results

One sentence was excluded from analysis because of a defect in the experiment. There was no sentence of which the error rate exceeded 20 % in any one of the stimuli sets. The mean correct response rate was 97.5%. The rate of correct responses in each condition is given in Table 5–3. Error responses were excluded from the subsequent analysis. The median of the correct response times from the word onset in each condition for each participant was calculated and the mean median times across conditions were compared.

The mean response time from the onset of shape words in each condition for each proficiency group is shown in Figure 5–4. The results of a three way analysis of variance (ANOVA) with two repeated-measure factors (the complexity factor and the fluency factor) and one between-groups factor (the proficiency

Table 5–3 Correct response rate of Chinese participants in each condition (%)

| Conditions | Novice | Intermediate | Expert |
|---|---|---|---|
| Simple | | | |
| Fluent | 98.6 | 96.1 | 98.6 |
| Filler | 97.2 | 96.3 | 94.9 |
| Pause | 96.6 | 98.9 | 97.5 |
| Complex | | | |
| Fluent | 97.8 | 98.3 | 96.7 |
| Filler | 98.3 | 98.1 | 97.8 |
| Pause | 97.8 | 97.8 | 98.3 |

factor) are given in Table 5–4. There were significant main effects of the complex factor and the fluency factor, $F(1, 33) = 12.95, p < .001$; $F(2, 66) = 4.88, p < .011$, respectively. Interactions between complexity-fluency factors and complexity-fluency-proficiency factors were also significant, $F(2, 66) = 11.20, p < .001$; $F(4, 66) = 2.51, p < .05$, respectively. We inspect the three way interaction by the proficiency factor.

In the novice group, there was a simple main effect of the complexity factor, $F(1, 33) = 13.76, p < .001$, but no simple main effect of the fluency factor, $F(2, 66) = .16, p = .85$. A simple interaction between complexity-fluency factors was not significant, $F(2, 66) = .063, p = .939$. No significant difference among conditions of the fluency factor was found either in the simple or the complex condition, $F(2, 132) = .104, p = .901$; $F(2, 132) = .103, p = .903$, respectively. Response times to complex phrases were significantly longer than response times to simple phrases in all the fluency conditions.

In the intermediate group, there were no simple main effects of the complexity and the fluency factors, $F(1, 33) = 2.35, p = .13$; $F(2, 66) = .69, p = .51$, respectively. A simple interaction between complexity-fluency factors was significant, $F(2, 66) = 10.23, p < .001$. Post-hoc tests revealed that there were significant differences among fluency conditions both in the simple and the complex conditions, $F(2, 132) = 4.07, p < .019$; $F(2, 132) = 8.62, p < .001$, respectively. Paired comparisons (alpha adjusted by Bonferroni) showed that response times to simple phrases were significantly shorter in the fluent condition than in the filler condition, $t(11) = 2.65, p < .037$, but there was no significant difference between fluent-pause conditions and filler-pause conditions, $t(11) = 2.11, p = .13$; $t(11) = 0.69, p = 1.00$, respectively. In contrast, response times to complex phrases were significantly shorter in the filler condition than in the fluent condition, $t(11) = 3.82, p < .002$. There was no significant difference between fluent-pause conditions or filler-pause conditions, $t(11) = 2.51, p = .052$; $t(11) = 1.73, p = .28$, respectively.

Table 5–4 Analysis of variance

| Source | df | MSe | F | p |
|---|---|---|---|---|
| Between subjects ||||| 
| Proficiency (P) | 2 | 505095.63 | 3.15 | .056 |
| error (P) | 33 | 160139.31 | | |
| Within subjects ||||| 
| Complexity (C) | 1 | 385810.14 | 12.95 | .001** |
| C × P | 2 | 61724.91 | 2.07 | .142 |
| error C (P) | 33 | 29800.47 | | |
| Fluency (F) | 2 | 5758.75 | 4.88 | .011* |
| F × P | 4 | 1716.35 | 1.46 | .226 |
| error F (P) | 66 | 1179.04 | | |
| C × F | 2 | 19169.35 | 11.20 | .001** |
| C × F × P | 4 | 4304.89 | 2.51 | .050* |
| error CF (P) | 66 | 1712.17 | | |

*$p < .05$. **$p < .01$.

In the expert group there was a significant simple main effect of the fluency factor, $F(2, 66) = 6.94, p < .002$, but no simple main effect of the complexity factor, $F(1, 33) = .98, p = .33$. A simple interaction between complexity-fluency factors was significant, $F(2, 66) = 5.93, p < .004$. Post-hoc tests revealed that there was a significant difference among fluency conditions in the complex condition, but not in the simple condition, $F(2, 132) = 12.00, p < .001; F(2, 132) = .64, p = .53$, respectively. Paired comparisons (alpha adjusted by Bonferroni) showed that response times to complex phrases were significantly shorter in the filler condition than in the fluent condition, $t(11) = 4.49, p < .001$. Response times to complex phrases in the pause condition were also significantly shorter than those in the fluent condition, $t(11) = 3.18, p < .01$. There was no significant difference between filler-pause conditions: $t(11) = 1.82, p = .23$.

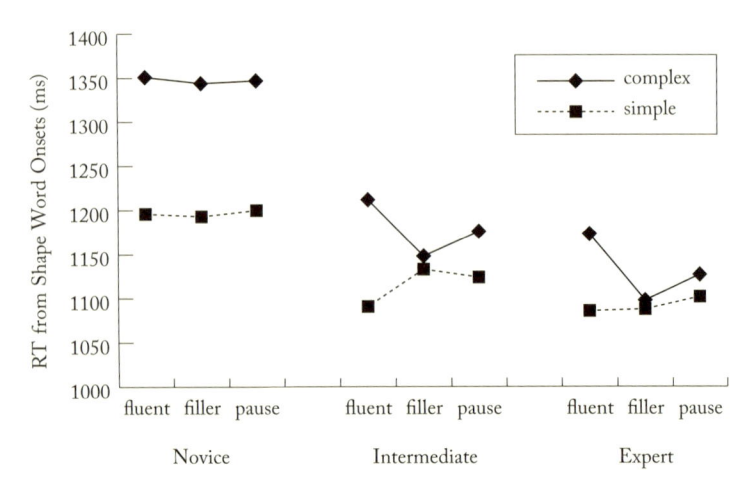

Figure 5–4 Novice, intermediate, and expert Chinese groups' mean response times to simple and complex phrases from the onsets of the words describing shapes in the fluent, filler and pause conditions.

### 5.4.5. Discussion

Chinese groups showed different response patterns depending on their proficiency in Japanese. The response pattern of the expert group was parallel to that of native Japanese, although the mean response time was 209ms longer than that of native listeners. Namely, the response times to complex phrases were shorter with preceding filled pauses than without any pauses, whereas there was no significant difference in response times to simple phrases between any conditions of the fluency factor. The results of the expert group agreed with our prediction, and supported the hypothesis. Response times to complex phrases in the silent pause condition were also shorter than those in the fluent condition, and there was no significant difference between filler-pause conditions. The expert group seemed to be utilising filled pauses at phrase boundaries just like native Japanese listeners.

In contrast with the expert group, the response pattern of the novice group was different from that of the Japanese listeners. Response times to complex phrases were simply longer than response times to simple phrases in all the fluency conditions, and no effects of filled or silent pauses were observed either in the simple or the complex condition. The hypothesis was not supported by this group. The novice group might have been unaware of the occurrence of filled pauses. Another possibility is that they were aware of the occurrence but had not realised that they were filled pauses, which they also had in their own language, and consequently were not utilising them like native or expert non-native listeners do. In any case, the results indicate that filled pauses at phrase boundaries neither help nor hinder the comprehension of Chinese speakers who have a good command of everyday Japanese and have stayed in Japan for 0.5–1.5 years.

The response pattern of the intermediate group is interesting in that it seems to reveal a transition stage of learners acquiring native like strategies for processing filled pauses. We pointed out that filled pauses before simple phrases might have negative effects because they tend to precede complex phrases. Filled pauses are not good cues to simple phrases. This seems to have happened to the intermediate group. Response times to simple phrases were longer with preceding filled pauses than without filled pauses. On the other hand, their responses to complex phrases were faster with preceding filled pauses than without, as with the case of the expert and Japanese groups. These results indicate that the listeners of this group were aware that filled pauses tend to precede complex phrases and expected a complex phrase after a filled pause. Consequently, when a complex phrase followed as expected, their responses were accelerated, whereas when a simple phrase followed a filled pause, their expectation was betrayed and their responses were delayed. The results of the intermediate group agreed with our prediction and supported the hypothesis.

In the intermediate group, response times to complex phrases in the silent pause condition did not significantly differ from those in the fluent condition.

Here, we observe the difference in the effects of silent pauses from those of filled pauses. Although there was no significant difference between filler-pause conditions in the complex condition, the difference between filler-fluent conditions was clearer than the difference between pause-fluent conditions in this group. This is also true with responses to simple phrases: While response times to simple phrases were significantly longer in the filler condition than in the fluent condition, there was no significant difference between the pause-fluent conditions. The results suggest that the sounds of filled pauses cue the complexity of the upcoming phrase more clearly than silence of the same duration because they signal explicitly the speakers' planning difficulties.

## 5.5. Chapter Summary

We tested the hypothesis generated from corpus-based studies that listeners expect a relatively long and complex phrase when there is a filled pause. Japanese speakers' response times to complex phrases were shorter when the phrases were preceded by a filled pause than when there was no pause, whereas no significant difference was found in response times to simple phrases between with and without filler conditions. These results supported the hypothesis and indicate that filled pauses at phrase boundaries can be cues to the complexity of the upcoming phrase. Our results agree with those of Arnold, Fagnano, and Tanenhaus (2003) and Bailey and Ferreira (2003) in that listeners are likely to be sensitive to co-occurrence of filled pauses and the type of following constituents. When the situational or linguistic contexts constrain the possible types of utterances to follow, listeners' expectations are biased by filled pauses toward the types which are more difficult for speakers to access or formulate and therefore take longer to plan. Our results are also in accordance with those of Fox Tree (2001)'s study on fillers in English and Dutch in that fillers do not disturb listener comprehension of speech but rather help it.

Chinese speakers' response patterns varied depending on their proficiency in spoken Japanese. Filled pauses had neither negative nor positive effects on those who had stayed in Japan for 0.5–1.5 years. However, in 1.5–2.5 years, Chinese speakers studying at Japanese universities seem to become aware of the forms and functions of filled pauses in Japanese and start utilizing them in communication in a way similar to that of native Japanese listeners. Those who have stayed in Japan for longer than 2.5 years seem to have the same strategies for processing filled pauses as those of Japanese listeners.

The results of Chinese speakers did not show any negative effects of filled pauses at phrase boundaries, either, except for the case of the second year group: Filled pauses before simple phrases delayed their responses. However, it is unlikely that the delay was caused because the listeners of this group did not recognise fillers as such, as Buck (2001) argued, but rather because they seemed to overgeneralise the tendency of filled pauses appearing before complex phrases. Positive effects of filled pauses before complex phrases would not have been observed if the listeners had not recognised fillers as fillers. These negative effects seem to reflect a stage of Chinese listeners acquiring the forms and the functions of filled pauses in the non-native language.

As our study was limited to the effects of one type of filler *eto*, we need to examine the effects of other types to understand the functions of filled pauses more comprehensively. However, as *ano* and *e* which are among the four frequent types of fillers, are also natural in this context, experiments using *ano* or *e* instead of *eto* are likely to result in similar findings.

We conjecture that filled pauses, repetitions and prolongations of function words, and the combination of those such as *theee um* and *and uh* in English can have similar effects to those of *eto* in this study. In Japanese, articles do not exist and function words are located after content words in constituents (e.g. postpositions instead of prepositions). Therefore, less function words are available as a time gaining device at the beginning of major constituents (Fox & Hayashi, 1996). Thus, filled pauses seem to play a more dominant role among other types of disfluencies in Japanese than in English.

It remains to be seen what effects filled pauses within accentual phrases have on listeners. When fillers are not delimited by silent pauses and compose parts of accentual phrases, it may be more difficult for listeners to identify them as fillers, particularly in case of *ano* and *sono*, both of which have functions as determiners as well as those of fillers. Consequently, fillers in such locations may cause negative effects.

In examining the effects of filled pauses on non-native listeners, a finer control of listeners' proficiency levels in the non-native language as well as the lengths of stay, particularly in the first two years after arrival, will be useful to obtain more fine-grained pictures of listeners acquiring skills of processing filled pauses in the non-native language. Research on the effects of disfluencies on non-native listeners is beneficial to gain insight into language universal and language specific aspects of disfluency processing as well as indispensable for studies of foreign language learning and teaching.

# Chapter 6

# Conclusion

## 6.1. Summary

We set forth the motivation, the purpose, and the scope of the study in Chapter 1. The purpose was to describe the features of filled pauses in Japanese and find out their roles in speech communication.

We surveyed the literature relevant to the present study in Chapter 2. We introduced the classification methods and typical features of disfluency types in Section 2.2. Section 2.3 referred to the features of filled pauses. In Section 2.4, we surveyed studies on speech production models and disfluencies. In Section 2.5, we referred to research on the effects of disfluencies on listeners with particular attention paid to filled pauses. From the survey, we proposed two hypotheses, "the boundary hypothesis" and "the complexity hypothesis." Both of the hypotheses were tested in Chapter 4.

Speaker variation is known to be large in disfluency production. In Chapter 3, we examined whether sociolinguistic factors such as speech levels and speaker attributes affect the choice of filler types. We conducted analyses of variance and clustering using the rates of prolongations and six common types of fillers in 240 presentations from *The Corpus of Spontaneous Japanese* (CSJ). In academic presentations, the most frequent type was *e*, whereas in casual presentations, the most common type was prolongations. Female speakers preferred *ano* and prolongations, whereas the favourite types among male speakers were *e, ma, sono* and vowel type fillers. *ano* and vowel type fillers were more frequent among older speakers, whereas *eto* are more common among younger generations. These results indicate that speech levels and speaker attributes affect the choice of disfluency types, and that the relevant factors differ depending on the type.

Studies on disfluency production in English and Dutch showed that filled pauses and repetitions are more frequent at deeper syntactic and discourse boundaries than at shallower ones. It was also found that the longer and more complex the constituent, the higher the disfluency rate at the beginning of it. However, there has hardly been any research about whether the same distributional features can be found in the other types of languages. We named "the boundary hypothesis" the view that disfluencies are more frequent at deeper boundaries. We call "the complexity hypothesis" the hypothesis that the longer and the more complex the constituent, the higher the disfluency rate at the beginning of constituent. In Chapter 4, we tested the two hypotheses by examining the filler rates at major syntactic and discourse boundaries in presentational speeches in CSJ. Boundary strengths had stronger effects on the filler rates than the complexity of the following clause. The effects of the complexity of the following clause were more obvious at shallower boundaries. The results are compatible with the view that speakers need to be engaged in more conceptual planning at deeper boundaries than at shallower ones. We speculated that speakers are able to plan only a limited number of linguistic units at deeper boundaries, because they first have to conceptualise a message and need time and attention for it. As a consequence, correspondence between the filler rate and the complexity of the following constituent becomes weaker. On the other hand, as less conceptual planning is required at shallower boundaries, the filler rates more clearly reflect the length or the complexity of the following linguistic unit to be planned.

In Chapter 5, we examined whether filled pauses affect listeners' predictions about the meaning of upcoming phrases. Research using spontaneous speech corpora shows that constituents tend to be longer or more complex when they are immediately preceded by filled pauses than when they are not. From this finding, we hypothesized that filled pauses cause listeners to expect that the speaker is going to refer to something that is likely to need a relatively long or complex expression. In the experiments, participants listened to sentences describing both simple and compound shapes on a computer screen. Their task was to press a button as soon as they had identified the shape corresponding to the description. Phrases describing shapes were immediately preceded by a filled pauses, a silent pause of the same duration, or no pause. We predicted that listeners' response times to compound shapes would be shorter when there is a filled pause before phrases describing the shape than when there is no filled pause, because filled pauses are good cues to complex phrases, whereas response times to simple shapes would not be shorter with a preceding filled pause than without. The results of native Japanese and proficient non-native Chinese listeners agreed with the prediction. The results indicate that native and proficient non-native listeners are making use of filled pauses as cues for the complexity of the following phrase. The time that filled pauses allow listeners seems a crucial factor for the listeners to predict the content of the upcoming speech. Response times of the least proficient non-native listeners were not affected by the existence of filled pauses, which suggests that the effects of filled pauses on non-native listeners depend on their language proficiency.

## 6.2. Contributions

The purpose of this thesis was to describe the features of filled pauses in Japanese and find out their roles in speech communication. From the point of speech production processes, we found some features common to English, Dutch, and Japanese filled pauses. The rates of filled pauses at major constituent boundaries are affected by the boundary strengths and the complexity of the following constituent. The filler rate tends to be higher at deeper boundaries and before longer or more complex constituents. These findings indicate language universal aspects of the occurrence of filled pauses.

We also found that filler rates are more weakly related to the complexity of the following constituent at stronger boundaries. We argued that the unit of linguistic encoding tends to be smaller than the unit of conceptual planning. The complexity of the following constituent seems to have more relevance to filler rates at the points at which less conceptual planning is required, i.e. shallower boundaries.

Another important contribution of this study is to have shown the effects of filled pauses on listeners, particularly on non-native listeners, as there had hardly been any empirical research on this topic. The results with both Japanese and Chinese speakers indicate that filled pauses at phrase boundaries positively affect speech processing of listeners. This finding is in accordance with the findings on English filled pauses. Our study has enabled cross-linguistic comparisons of the effects of filled pauses on listeners between different types of languages. The results with Chinese speakers indicate that the effects of filled pauses in foreign languages depend on the listeners' proficiency level in the language.

It was also revealed that speakers' choice of types of disfluencies is affected by sociolinguistic factors such as speech levels and speakers' gender and age.

We have illustrated the distributional features of filled pauses in Japanese across speakers and within speeches, which had not been studied before. This study has added some knowledge about factors affecting the usage of filled pauses. The study has also provided some evidence to support the viewpoint that filled pauses at phrase boundaries help listeners' prediction about the content of the upcoming speech. Thus, the purpose of the thesis has been achieved.

## 6.3. Future Work

Various strategies are possible to achieve smooth communication, as Clark (1994) pointed out, and disfluencies are one of the strategies. In the present study, we investigated the features and roles of filled pauses, the most frequent type of disfluencies in Japanese. More detailed analyses of filled pauses, acoustic features and type dependent characteristics of them, for example, will surely contribute to better understanding of their roles in speech communication. Future work should also include research on the other types of disfluencies and the relationship among them.

Another important work is to investigate the features and the roles of disfluencies in dialogues, because dialogues are the most typical mode of communication. A large dialogue corpus will be indispensable for such research.

Not many studies have been conducted about the effects of disfluencies on listeners. Perception studies are possible with ingenuity of researchers, without a large database. New research equipments such as eye-trackers and fMRI (functional magnetic resonance imaging) will surely broaden the scope of disfluency studies.

Difficulties in processing disfluencies in a foreign language may depend on distance between one's own language and the foreign language. Presumably, it is easier to cope with disfluencies of a language similar to one's own than to process those of distant languages. Disfluency studies which include the ideas of language typology will surely provide useful insights for foreign language teaching and learning.

There will be other sociolinguistic factors, besides those examined in Chapter 3, which may affect speakers' choice of disfluency types; regional and social dialects, and relationship between the interlocutors, for example. Studies concerning such sociolinguistic variables will enrich the understanding of the roles of disfluencies.

Finally, further research on the acoustic features of disfluencies will improve the user-friendliness of dialogue systems. Disfluencies are intrinsic in any natural language. Therefore, if the systems allow users to be uncertain and disfluent, it will be much easier for the people, particularly for those who are not familiar with computer systems, to utilise such systems.

# Bibliography

Aaronson, D. (1968). Temporal course of perception in an immediate recall task. *Journal of Experimental Psychology*, 76, 129–140.

Araki, M., Itoh, T., Kumagai, T., & Ishizaki, M. (1999). Proposal of a standard utterance-unit tagging scheme. *Journal of Japanese Society for Artificial Intelligence*, 14(2), 251–260 (in Japanese).

Arnold, J. E., Altmann, R., Fagnano, M., & Tanenhaus, M. K. (2004). The Old and Thee, uh, New. *Psychological Science*, 578–582.

Arnold, J., E., Fagnano, M., & Tanenhaus, M. K. (2003a). Disfluencies signal theee, um, new information. *Journal of Psycholinguistic Research*, 32(1), 25–36.

Arnold, J., E., Altman, B., & Tanenhaus, M. K. (2003b). Disfluency isn't just um and uh: the role of prosody in the comprehension of disfluency. Abstract in CUNY 2003.

Bailey, K. G. D., & Ferreira, F. (2003). Disfluencies Affect the Parsing of Garden-Path Sentences. *Journal of Memory and Language*, 49, 183–200.

Barr, D. j. (2001). Trouble in mind: Paralinguistic indices of effort and uncertainty in communication. In C. Cave & I. Guaitella & S. Santi (Eds.), *Oralite et gestualite: Interactions et comportements multimodaux dans la communication*, 597–600. Paris: L'Harmattan.

Beattie, G. (1977). The dynamics of interruption and the filled pauses. *British Journal of Social and Clinical Psychology* 16, 283–284.

Beattie, G. (1979). Planning units in spontaneous speech: Some evidence from hesitation in speech and speaker gaze direction in conversation. *Linguistics*, 17, 61–78.

Blau, E. K. (1990). The effect of syntax, speed, and pauses on listening comprehension, *TESL Quarterly*, 16(4), 746–752.

Blau, E. K. (1991). More on comprehensible input: The effect of pauses and hesitation markers on listening comprehension. From *ERIC database*. Paper presented at the Annual Meeting of the Puerto Rico Teachers of English to Speakers of Other Languages (San Juan, PR, November 15, 1991).

Boomer, D. S. (1965). Hesitation and grammatical encoding, *Language and Speech*, 8, 148–158.

Bortfeld, H., Leon, S. D., Bloom, J. E., Schober, M. F., & Brennan, S. E. (2001). Disfluency Rates in Conversation: Effects of Age, Relationship, Topic, Role, and Gender. *Language and Speech*, 44(2), 123–147.

Brennan, S., E., & Schober, M. (2001). How listeners compensate for disfluencies in spontaneous speech. *Journal of Memory and Language*, 44, 274–296.

Brennan, S., E. & Williams, M. (1995). The feeling of another's knowing: prosody and filled pauses as cues to listeners about the metacognitive states of speakers. *Journal of Memory and Language* 34, 383–398.

Brinton, L. J. (1996). *Pragmatic markers in English: grammaticalization and discourse functions*. Berlin: Mouton de Gruyter.

Broen, P. A., & Siegel, G. M. (1972). Variations in normal speech disfluencies. *Language and Speech*, 15(3), 219–231.

Brown, G. (1977). *Listening to spoken English*. London: Longman.

Buck, G. (2001). *Assessing listening*. Cambridge University Press, Cambridge.

Chafe, W. (1980). The deployment of consciousness in the production of a narrative, in Chafe, W. (ed.) *The Pear Stories, Cognitive, Cultural, and Linguistic Aspects of Narrative Production*, 9–50. ABLEX Publishing Corporation, Norwood, New Jersey.

Chiang, C. S., & Dunkel, P. (1992). The effect of speech modification, prior knowledge, and listening proficiency on EFL lecture learning. *TESOL Quarterly*, 26(2), 345–374.

Christenfeld, N. (1994). Options and Ums. *Journal of Language and Social Psychology* 113(2), 192–199.

Christenfeld, N. (1996). Effects of a metronome on the filled pauses of fluent speakers. *Journal of Speech and Hearing Research*, 39(6), 1232–1238.

Christenfeld, N. & Creger, B. (1996). Anxiety, alcohol, aphasia and ums. *Journal of Personality and Social Psychology*, 70, 451–460.

Christenfeld, N., Schachter, S. & Bilous, F. (1991). Filled Pauses and Gestures: It's Not Coincidence. *Journal of Psycholinguistic Research*, 20(1), 1–10.

Clark, H. H. (1994). Managing problems in speaking. *Speech Communication*, 15, 243–250.

Clark, H. H. (2002). Speaking in time. *Speech Communication*, 36, 5–13.

Clark, H. H. & Fox Tree, J. E. (2002). Using *uh* and *um* in spontaneous speaking, *Cognition*, 84, 73–111.

Clark, H. H. & Wasow, T. (1998). Repeating words in spontaneous speech. *Cognitive Psychology*, 37, 201–242.

Cook, M. (1971). The incidence of filled pauses in relation to part of speech. *Language and Speech*, 14(2), 135–139.

Cook, M., Smith, J., & Lalljee, M. G. (1974). Filled pauses and syntactic complexity. *Language and Speech*, 17(1), 11–16.

Cristal, D. (2003). *A Dictionary of Linguistics & Phonetics*. Blackwell Publishing, Oxford, UK.

Cutler, A., Dahan, D., & van Donselaar, W. (1997). Prosody in the comprehension of spoken language: a literature review. *Language and Speech* 40 (2), 141–201.

Fayer, J., & Krasinski, E. (1987). Native and nonnative Judgment of intelligibility and irritation, *Language Learning,* 37(3), 313–326.
Finegan, E. (1994). *Language: its structure and use.* New York: Harcourt Brace.
Fleiss, J. L. (1971). Measuring nominal scale agreement among many raters. *Psychological Bulletin,* 76, 378–382.
Flowerdew, J. (1994). Research of relevance to second language lecture comprehension - an overview, in *Academic Listening,* Flowerdew, J. (Ed.), 7–29. Cambridge: Cambridge University Press.
Flowerdew, J., & Miller, L. (1992). Student perceptions, problems and strategies in L2 lectures. *RELC Journal,* 23(2), 60–80.
Foulke, E., & Sticht, T. G. (1969). Review of research on the intelligibility and comprehension of accelerated speech. *Psychological Bulletin,* 72, 59–62.
Fox, B. A., Hayashi, M., & Jasperson, R., (1996). Resource and repair: a cross linguistic study of syntax and repair, in Ochs, Schegloff, E., A., &. Thompson, S. A., (Eds.), *Interaction and Grammar,* 185–237. Cambridge: Cambridge University Press.
Fox Tree, J. E. (1995). The effects of false starts and repetitions on the processing of subsequent words in spontaneous speech. *Journal of Memory and Language,* 34, 709–738.
Fox Tree, J. E. (2001). Listeners' uses of *um* and *uh* in speech comprehension. *Memory and Cognition,* 29 (2), 320–326.
Fox Tree, J. E., (2002). Interpreting pauses and *um*s at turn exchanges. *Discourse Processes,* 34(1), 37–55.
Fukao, Y., Mizuta, S., & Ohtsubo, K. (1991). Development of teaching material for advanced learners of Japanese to improve their listening skills for lecture comprehension. Paper presented at the Autumn Meeting of the Society for Teaching Japanese as a Foreign Language (in Japanese).
Goldman-Eisler, F. (1968). *Psycholinguistics.* London: Academic Press.
Goldman-Eisler, F. (1972). Pauses, clauses, sentences. *Language and Speech,* 15(2), 103–113.
Goto, M., Itou K., & Hayamizu, S. (1999). A real-time system detecting filled pauses in spontaneous speech. *Information Processing Society of Japan SIG Notes* 99 (64), 9–16 (in Japanese).
Goto, M., Itou, K., & Hayamizu, S. (2002). Speech completion: on-demand completion assistance using filled pauses for speech input interfaces, *Proceedings of the 7th International Conference on Spoken Language Processing,* 1489–1492.
Griffiths, R. (1990). Speech rate and NNS comprehension: a preliminary study in time-benefit analysis. *Language Learning,* 40(3), 311–336.
Griffiths, R. (1991). Pausological research in an L2 context: A rationale, and review of selected studies. *Applied Linguistics,* 12(4), 345–364.

Griffiths, R., & Beretta, A. (1991). A controlled study of temporal variables in NS-NNS lectures. *RELC Journal*, 22(1), 1–19.

Hakoda, K. & Soto, H. (1975). A pause insertion rule for connected speech. *Transactions on Technical Committee of the Acoustical Society of Japan*, March, 1975, 1–7 (in Japanese).

Hawkins, P.R. (1971). The syntactic location of hesitation pauses. *Language and Speech*, 14, 277–288.

Hirschberg, J. & Nakatani, C. H. (1996). A prosodic analysis of discourse segments in direction-giving monologues. In *Proceedings of the 34th annual meeting of the association for computational linguistics*, 286–293.

Holmes, V. M. (1988). Hesitations and sentence planning. *Language and cognitive processes*, 3(4), 323–361.

Holmes, V. M. (1995) A crosslinguistic comparison of the production of utterances in discourse. *Cognition*, 54, 169–207.

Ishizaki, M., & Den, Y. (2001). *Discourse and dialogue*. University of Tokyo press: Tokyo (in Japanese).

Itagaki, T., Shinoda, K., & Sagayama, S. (2002). Language modelling using speaker dependency of fillers for spontaneous speech recognition. *Proceedings of the Second Spontaneous Speech Science and Technology Workshop*, Tokyo, 79–84 (in Japanese).

Ito, T., Minematsu, N., & Nakagawa, S. (1995). Analysis of filled pauses and their use in a dialogue system. *The Journal of Acoustical Society of Japan*, 55 (5), 333–342 (in Japanese).

Kaiki, N. & Sagisaka, Y. (1996). Study of pause insertion rules based on local phrase dependency structure. *The Transactions of the Institute of Electronics, Information and Communication Engineers*, Vol.J79-D-2, No.9, 1455–1463 (in Japanese).

Kawamori, K, & Shimazu, A. (1996). On the form and function of Japanese discourse markers. *IEICE technical report. Natural language understanding and models of communication*, 96(46), 27–32 (in Japanese).

Kempen, G. & Hoenkamp E. (1987). An incremental procedural grammar for sentence formulation. Cognitive Science, 11, 201–258.

Koide, K. (1983). Hesitation, in *Lecture Series of Japanese Expression 3: Expressions in Speech* pp. 81–87. Mizutani, Y. (Ed.) Chikumashobou, Tokyo (in Japanese).

Koiso, H., Nishikawa, K., & Mabuchi, Y. (2006). Transcription, in *Construction of The Corpus of Spontaneous Japanese*, 23–132. The National Institute for Japanese Language (in Japanese).

Levelt, W. J. M. (1989). *Speaking*. The MIT Press, Cambridge, Massachusetts.

Lickley, R.J. (1994). Detecting Disfluency in Spontaneous Speech. Doctoral dissertation, University of Edinburgh.

Lounsbury, F. G. (1954). Transitional probability, linguistic structure, and systems of habit-

family hierarchies. In *Psycholinguistics: A Survey of Theory and Research Problems*, 93–101. Osgood, C. E. and Sebeod, T. A. (eds.) Waverly Press: Baltimore.

Maclay, H., Osgood, C. E. (1959). Hesitation phenomena in spontaneous English speech. *Word*, 15, 19–44.

Maekawa, K. (2002). Compilation of the Corpus of Spontaneous Japanese: A status Report, *Proceedings of the Second Spontaneous Speech Science and Technology Workshop*, Tokyo, 7–10 (in Japanese).

Maekawa, K. (2004). Design, Compilation, and Some Preliminary Analyses of the Corpus of Spontaneous Japanese. In Yoneyama, K. and Maekawa, K. (Eds.). *Spontaneous Speech: Data and Analysis*. Tokyo: The National Institute for Japanese Language, 87–108.

Maekawa, K. (2005). Spontaneous speech and speech database. *The Journal of Acoustical Society of Japan, 61* (9), 544–549 (in Japanese).

Mahl, G. F. (1956). Disturbances and silences in the patient's speech in psychotherapy. *Journal of Abnormal and Social Psychology* 53, 1–15.

Minami, F. (1974). *Gendai nihongo no kouzou* (The structure of modern Japanese). Taisyukan syoten, Tokyo (in Japanese).

Minami, F. (1993). *Gendai nihongo bunpou no Rinkaku* (The profile of the modern Japanese grammar), Taisyukan syoten, Tokyo (in Japanese).

Murakami, J. & Sagayama, S. (1991). A discussion of acoustic and linguistic problems in spontaneous speech recognition. *Technical Report of IEICE, SP91–100, NLC91–57*, 71–78 (in Japanese).

Nakagawa, S., & Kobayasi, S. (1995). Phenomena and acoustic variation on interjections, pauses, and repairs in spontaneous speech. *Journal of the Acoustical Society of Japan*, 51(3), 202–212 (in Japanese).

Niimura, I (ed.) (1998). *Koujien*, the fifth edition. Iwanami Shoten, Tokyo (in Japanese).

Noda, H. (1986). Modification of *wa* and *ga* in complex sentences. *Nihongogaku*, 5(2), 31–43 (in Japanese).

Reich, S. S. (1980). Significance of pauses for speech perception. *Journal of Psycholinguistic Research*, 9(4), 379–389.

Reynolds, A., & Paivio, A. (1968). Cognitive and emotional determinants of speech. *Canadian Journal of Psychology*, 22, 164–175.

Rochester, S. R. (1973). The significance of pauses in spontaneous speech. *Journal of Psycholinguistic Research*, 2, 51–81.

Rose, R. L. (1998). *The Communicative Value of Filled Pauses in Spontaneous Speech*. Unpublished MA thesis at University of Birmingham.

Rubin, J., (1994). A Review of Second Language Listening Comprehension Research. *The Modern Language Journal*, 78, 199–221.

Sadanobu, T., & Takubo, Y. (1995). The monitoring, devices of mental operations in discourse – a case of 'eeto' and 'ano (o)' – . *Gengo Kenkyu,* 108, 74–93 (in Japanese).

Schachter, S., Christenfeld, N., Ravina,B.,& Bilous, F. (1991). Speech disfluency and the structure of knowledge. *Journal of Personality and Social Psychology*, 60, 362–367.

Schiffrin, D. (1987). *Discourse markers.* Cambridge: Cambridge University Press.

Shiozawa, T. (1979). A survey on hesitations in Japanese. in *Hidden dimensions of communication*, Peng, F., C., C., (Ed.). Bunka Hyoron Publishing Company, Hiroshima, Japan (in Japanese).

Shriber, E.E. (1994). *Preliminaries to a theory of speech disfluencies.* Unpublished Ph.D. thesis, University of California at Berkeley.

Shriberg, E. E. (2001). To "errrr" is human: ecology and acoustics of speech disfluencies. *Journal of the International Phonetic Association* 31(1), 153–169, Cambridge University Press.

Shriberg, E. E. (2005). Spontaneous speech: How people really talk, and why engineers should care. *Proceedings of Interspeech* 2005, 1781–1784.

Shriberg, E. E., Wade, E. & Price, P. J. (1992). Human-machine problem solving using spoken language systems (SLS): Factors affecting performance and user satisfaction. *Proc. DARPA Speech and Natural Language Workshop,* M. Marcus, (ed.), 49–54. Harriman, NY.

Smith, V.L. & Clark, H.H. (1993). On the course of answering questions. *Journal of Memory and Language,* 32, 25–38.

Sternberg, S., Monsell, S, Knoll, R.L., & Wright, C.E. (1978). The latency and duration of rapid movement sequences: Comparisons of speech and typing. In G. E. Stelmach (Ed.) *Information Processing in Motor Control and Learning.* New York: Academic Press, 117–152.

Stenstroem, A. (1994). *An Introduction to Spoken Interaction.* Longman: London and New York.

Sugito, M. (1990). On the role of pauses in production and perception of discourse. *Proceedings of the 1st International Conference on Spoken Language Processing,* 513–516, Kobe, Japan.

Sugito, M. (1994). *Voice of the Japanese,* Izumi shoin, Osaka, Japan (in Japanese).

Swerts, M., Wichmann, A. & Beun, R. (1996). Filled pauses as markers of discourse structure, *Proceedings of the 3rd International Conference on Spoken Language Processing*, 1033–1036.

Swerts, M. (1997). Prosodic features at discourse boundaries of different strength. *Journal of Acoustical Society of America,* 101 (1), 514–521.

Swerts, M. (1998). Filled pauses as markers of discourse structure. *Journal of Pragmatics,* 30, 485–496.

Takanashi, K., Maruyama, T., Uchimoto, K., & Isahara, H. (2003). Identification of sentences in spontaneous Japanese –Detection and modification of clause boundaries–. *Proceedings*

of *ISCA & IEEE Workshop on Spontaneous SpeechPprocessing and Recognition*, 183–186.
Takanashi, K., Uchimoto, K., & Maruyama, T. (2004). Identification of clause units in CSJ. In vol.1, *The Corpus of Spontaneous Japanese* (in Japanese).
Takubo, Y. (1987). Syntactic structure and contextual information, *Nihongogaku*, 6 (5), 37–48 (in Japanese).
Takubo, Y. & Kinsui, S. (1997). The function of responses and interjections in discourse. *Speech and Grammar*, pp. 257–279. Spoken Language Working Group (Ed.) Kuroshioshuppan: Tokyo (in Japanese).
Tanaka, H. (1988). *Seibido's dictionary of linguistics*. Seibido, Tokyo (in Japanese).
Taylor, I. (1969). Content and structure in sentence production. *Journal of Verbal Learning & Verbal Behavior*, 8(2), 170–175.
The National Institute for Japanese Language. (2006). *Construction of The Corpus of Spontaneous Japanese*, The National Institute for Japanese Language.
The National Institute for Japanese Language (NIJLA) & The National Institute of Communications Technology (NICT) (2004). *The Corpus of Spontaneous Japanese*.
Uchimoto, K., Maruyama, T., Takanashi, K., & Isahara, H. (2004). The manual for labeling modifying structures in *The Corpus of Spontaneous Japanese* (in Japanese).
Venditti, J. (1995). Japanese ToBI labeling guideline. http://ling.ohio-state.edu/phonetics/J_ToBI/
Voss, B. (1979). Hesitation phenomena as sources of perceptual errors for non-native speakers. *Language and Speech*, 22(2), 129–44.
Wasow, T. (1997). Remarks on grammatical weight. *Language Variation and Change*, 9, 81–105.
Wasow, T. (2002). *Postverbal Behavior*. CSLI Publications, Stanford, California.
Watanabe, M. (2001). An analysis of usage of fillers in Japanese Lecture-style speech. *Proceedings of the Spontaneous Speech Science and Technology Workshop*, Tokyo, 69–76(in Japanese).
Watanabe, M. (2002). Fillers as indicators of discourse segment boundaries in Japanese monologues. *Proceedings of Speech Prosody 2002*, Aix-en-Provence, France, 691–694 .
Watanabe, M. (2003). The constituent complexity and types of fillers in Japanese. *The Proceedings of the 15th International Congress of Phonetic Sciences*, 2473–2476, Barcelona, Spain.
Watanabe, M., Den, Y., Hirose, K., & Minematsu, N. (2004a). Clause types and filled pauses in Japanese spontaneous monologues. *Proceedings of the 8th International Conference on Spoken Language Processing*, 905–908. Jeju Island, Korea.
Watanabe, M., Den, Y., Hirose K., & Minematsu, N. (2004b). Types of clause boundaries and the frequencies of filled pauses. *Proceedings of the 18th General Meeting of the Phonetic Society of Japan*, 65–70 (in Japanese).

Watanabe, M., Hirose K., Den, Y., & Minematsu, N. (2006). The effects of filled pauses on listeners' prediction about the complexity of the following phrase. *The Journal of the Acoustical Society of Japan,* 62(5), 370–378 (in Japanese).

Watanabe, M., & Ishi, C. T. (2000). The distribution of fillers in lectures in the Japanese language. *Proceedings of the 6th International Conference on Spoken Language Processing,* Vol. 3, 167–170. Beijing, China.

Wu, C. H. & Yan, G. L. (2004). Acoustic feature analysis and discriminative modeling of filled pauses for spontaneous speech recognition. *The Journal of VLSI Signal Processing* Volume 36, Numbers 2–3, 91–104.

Yamane, C. (2002). *Nihongo no Danwa ni Okeru Firaa (Fillers in Japanese Discourse),* Kurosio Syuppan: Tokyo (in Japanese).

Yokobayashi, H. (1994). What are the functions of "eto," "ano," "ma", and "e"? *The Monthly Nihongo,* 5, 68–69 (in Japanese).

# List of Relevant Publications

Watanabe, M. (1999). The distribution of filled pauses in the university lectures. *Proceedings of the 13th General Meeting of the Phonetic Society of Japan,* 143–148 (in Japanese).

Watanabe, M. (2000). The distribution of fillers in Japanese-language lectures. *Proceedings of the Spring Meeting of the Acoustical Society of Japan,* 199–200 (in Japanese).

Watanabe, M., & Ishii, C. T. (2000). The distribution of fillers in lectures in the Japanese language. *Proceedings of the 6th International Conference on Spoken Language Processing,* Vol.3, 167–170. Beijing, China.

Watanabe, M. (2001a). An analysis of usage of fillers in Japanese Lecture-style speech. *Proceedings of the Spontaneous Speech Science and Technology Workshop,* Tokyo, 69–76 (in Japanese).

Watanabe, M. (2001b). The usage of fillers at discourse segment boundaries in Japanese lecture-style monologues. *Proceedings of ISCA Tutorial and research workshop, Disfluency in Spontaneous Speech,* 89–92. Edinburgh, UK.

Watanabe, M. (2001c). The frequencies of filled pauses at discourse segment boundaries in lectures. *Proceedings of the 15th General Meeting of the Phonetic Society of Japan,* 85–90 (in Japanese).

Watanabe, M. (2001d). Acoustic features of fillers and connectives at discourse segment boundaries in Japanese monologues. *Proceedings of the Autumn Meeting of the Acoustical Society of Japan,* 277–278 (in Japanese).

Watanabe, M. (2002a). Fillers as Discourse Segment Boundary Markers in Japanese Monologues. *Bulletin of Foreign Language Teaching Association*, 6, 13–24. Foreign Language Teaching Association, University of Tokyo.

Watanabe, M. (2002b). Fillers and Connectives as Discourse Segment Boundary Markers in an Academic Monologue in Japanese. *Bulletin of International Center,* 12, 107–119, International Center, The University of Tokyo.

Watanabe, M. (2002c). The function of filled pauses as discourse segment boundary markers in Japanese monologues. *Proceedings of ISCA Workshop on Temporal Integration in the Perception of Speech,* 51. Aix-en-Provence, France.

Watanabe, M. (2002d). Fillers as indicators of discourse segment boundaries in Japanese monologues. *Proceedings of Speech Prosody 2002,* 691–694. Aix-en-Provence, France.

Watanabe, M. (2002e). Classification of simulated public speeches based on the frequencies of filler types. *Proceedings of the 16th General Meeting of the Phonetic Society of Japan*, 145–150 (in Japanese).

Watanabe, M., & Den, Y., (2003). When and why do speakers prolong their speech segments? *Proceedings of the 1st JST/CREST International Workshop on Expressive Speech Processing*, 71–74. Kobe, Japan

Watanabe, M. (2003). The constituent complexity and types of fillers in Japanese. *The Proceedings of the 15th International Congress of Phonetic Sciences*, 2473–2476, Barcelona, Spain.

Watanabe, M., Den, Y., Hirose, K., & Minematsu, N. (2004a). Clause types and filled pauses in Japanese spontaneous monologues. *Proceedings of the 8th International Conference on Spoken Language Processing*, 905–908. Jeju Island, Korea.

Watanabe, M., Den, Y., Hirose K., & Minematsu, N. (2004b). Types of clause boundaries and the frequencies of filled pauses. *Proceedings of the 18th General Meeting of the Phonetic Society of Japan*, 65–70 (in Japanese).

Watanabe, M., Den, Y., Hirose K., & Minematsu, N. (2004c). Effects of filled pauses on listeners' expectation about the complexity of upcoming phrases. *Proceedings of the Autumn Meeting of the Acoustical Society of Japan*, vol. 1, 463–464 (in Japanese).

Watanabe, M., Den, Y., Hirose, K., & Minematsu, N. (2005a). Effects of silent and filled pauses at clause boundaries on non-native listeners' comprehension of speech, *Proceedings of the Spring Meeting of the Acoustical Society of Japan*, 325–326 (in Japanese).

Watanabe, M., Hirose, K., Den, Y., & Minematsu, N. (2005b). Filled Pauses as Cues to the Complexity of Following Phrases. *Proceedings of Interspeech 2005*, 37–40, Lisbon, Portugal.

Watanabe, M., Den, Y., Hirose, K., & Minematsu, N. (2005c). Effects of filled pauses on native and non-native listeners' speech processing, *Proceedings of the ISCA Tutorial and Research Workshop, Disfluency in Spontaneous Speech*, 169–172, Aix-en-Provence, France.

Watanabe, M., Hirose, K., Den, Y., & Minematsu, N. (2005d). The effects of filled pauses at phrase boundaries on listeners' predictions, *Proceedings of the 19th General Meeting of the Phonetic Society of Japan*, 37–42, (in Japanese).

Watanabe, M., Den, Y., Hirose K., & Minematsu, N. (2005e). The effects of types and lengths of adjacent clauses on the ratios of filled pauses at clause boundaries, *Proceedings of the Autumn Meeting of the Acoustical Society of Japan*, 319–320 (in Japanese).

Watanabe, M., Hirose K., Den, Y., & Minematsu, N. (2006a). The effects of filled pauses on listeners' prediction about the complexity of the following phrase. *The Journal of the Acoustical Society of Japan*, 62(5), 370–378 (in Japanese).

Watanabe, M., Hirose, K., Den, Y., & Minematsu, N. (2006b). Factors influencing ratios of filled pauses at clause boundaries in Japanese, *Proceedings of ISCA Tutorial and Research Workshop on Experimental Linguistics*, 253–256. Athens, Greece.

Watanabe, M., Den, Y., Hirose, K., Miwa, S., & Minematsu, N. (2006c). Factors Affecting Speakers' Choice of Fillers in Japanese Presentations, *Proceedings of the 9th International Conference on Spoken Language Processing (Interspeech 2006)*, 1256–1259. Pittsburgh, USA.

Watanabe, M., Hirose, K., Den, Y., Inagaki, T., & Minematsu, N. (2007a). Clustering of academic presentations based on frequent filler types in Japanese, *Proceedings of the Spring Meeting of the Acoustical Society of Japan*, 303–304 (in Japanese).

Watanabe, M., Den, Y., Hirose, K., Miwa, S., & Minematsu, N. (2007b). Features of pauses and conjunctions at syntactic and discourse boundaries in Japanese monologues. *Proceedings of 10th European Conference on Speech Communication and Technology (Interspeech 2007)*, 118–121. Antwerp, Belgium.

Watanabe, M., Hirose, K., Den, Y., & Minematsu, N. (2008). Filled pauses as cues to the complexity of upcoming phrases for native and non-native listeners. *Speech Communication* 50, 81–94.

# 参考文献

[日本語]

荒木雅弘, 伊藤敏彦, 熊谷智子, 石崎雅人(1999)「発話単位タグ標準化案の作成」『人工知能学会誌』14(2), 251–260.

石崎雅人, 伝康晴(2001)『言語と計算 3 談話と対話』東京大学出版会

内元清貴, 丸山岳彦, 高梨克也, 井佐原均(2004)『『日本語話し言葉コーパス』における係り受け構造付与(Version 1.0)』『日本語話し言葉コーパス』Vol.1.

板垣貴裕, 篠田浩一, 嵯峨山茂樹(2002)「話し言葉音声の認識における間投詞の話者性を考慮した言語モデル」『第 2 回話し言葉の科学と工学ワークショップ講演予稿集』79–84.

伊藤敏彦, 峯松信明, 中川聖一(1999)「間投詞の働きの分析とシステム応答生成における間投詞の利用と評価」『日本音響学会誌』55(5), 333–342.

海木延佳, 匂坂芳典「局所的な句構造によるポーズ挿入規則化の検討」『電子情報通信学会論文誌. D-II』No.9, 1455–1463.

川森雅仁, 島津明(1996)「談話標識語の形式と機能について」『電子情報通信学会技術研究報告. NLC, 言語理解とコミュニケーション』96(46), 27–32.

小磯花絵, 西川賢哉, 間淵洋子(2006)「転記テキスト」『日本語話し言葉コーパスの構築法』23–132. 国立国語研究所

小出慶一(1983)「言いよどみ」『講座日本語の表現 3 話しことばの表現』81–87. 水谷修(編) 筑摩書房

国立国語研究所(2006)『日本語話し言葉コーパスの構築法』

国立国語研究所, 情報通信研究機構(2004)『日本語話し言葉コーパス』

後藤真孝, 伊藤克亘, 速水悟(1999)「自然発話中の言い淀み箇所のリアルタイム検出システム」『情報処理学会 音声言語情報処理研究会 研究報告』99-SLP-27-2, 99(64), 9–16.

定延利之, 田窪行則(1995)「談話における心的操作モニター機構」『言語研究』108, 74–93.

塩沢孝子(1979)「日本語の Hesitation に関する一考察」F. C. パン編『ことばの諸相』151–166. 文化評論出版

杉藤美代子(1994)『日本語音声の研究 1 日本人の声』和泉書院

高梨克也, 内元清貴, 丸山岳彦(2004)「『日本語話し言葉コーパス』における節単位認定 Version 1.0」『日本語話し言葉コーパス』Vol.1.

田窪行則 (1987)「統語構造と文脈情報」『日本語学』6 (5)，37–48. 明治書院
田窪行則，金水敏 (1997)「応答詞・感動詞の談話的機能」『文法と音声』257–279. 音声文法研究会編 くろしお出版
竹内和広，森本郁代，高梨克也，井佐原均 (2004)「『日本語話し言葉コーパス』の談話境界情報について Version 1.0」『日本語話し言葉コーパス』Vol.1.
田中春美編 (1988)『現代言語学辞典』成美堂
中川聖一，小林聡 (1995)「自然な音声対話における間投詞・ポーズ・言い直しの出現パターンと音響的性質」『日本音響学会誌』51 (3)，202–210.
野田尚史 (1986)「複文における「は」と「が」の係り方」『日本語学』5-2, 31–43.
箱田和雄，佐藤大和 (1975)「文音声のポーズ挿入規則」『日本音響学会音声研究会資料』1–7.
深尾百合子，水田澄子，大坪一夫 (1991)「講義講演理解能力の養成をめざした上級聴解教材開発」『平成3年度日本語教育学会秋季大会研究発表要旨』37–42.
前川喜久雄 (2002)「『日本語話し言葉コーパス』構築作業の現状と展望」『第2回話し言葉の科学と工学ワークショップ講演予稿集』7–11.
前川喜久雄 (2005)「自発音声とデータベース」『日本音響学会誌』61 (9)，544–549.
南不二男 (1974)『現代日本語の構造』大修館書店
南不二男 (1993)『現代日本語文法の輪郭』大修館書店
村上仁一，嵯峨山茂樹 (1991)「自由発話音声認識における音響的および言語的な問題点の検討」『電子情報通信学会技術研究報告 . NLC』SP91-100, NLC91-57, 71–78.
渡辺美知子 (2001)「講義・講演音声におけるフィラーの種類と出現傾向について」『話し言葉の科学と工学ワークショップ講演予稿集』69–76.
渡辺美知子，伝康晴，広瀬啓吉，峯松信明 (2004)「節境界の種類とフィラーの出現頻度」『第18回日本音声学会全国大会予稿集』65–70.
渡辺美知子，広瀬啓吉，伝康晴，峯松信明 (2006)「音声聴取時のフィラーの働き―「エート」による後続句の複雑さ予測―」『日本音響学会誌』62 (5)，370–378.
山根智恵 (2002)『日本語の談話におけるフィラー』くろしお出版
横196宙世 (1994)「『エート』『アノー』『マー』『エー』その働きと用法は？」『月刊日本語』1994年5月号, 68–69.

# 関連発表文献

[日本語]

渡辺美知子(1999)「フィラーの機能」『東京大学外国語教育学研究会研究論集』第3号，38–47．東京大学外国語教育学研究会

渡辺美知子(1999)「講義の発話におけるフィラーの分布」『第13回日本音声学会全国大会予稿集』143–148.

渡辺美知子(2000)「日本語の講義開始部におけるフィラーの分布」『言語情報科学研究』第5号，283–301.東京大学言語情報科学研究会

渡辺美知子(2000)「講義音声におけるフィラーの分布」『日本音響学会2000年春季研究発表会講演論文集Ⅰ』199–200.

渡辺美知子(2001)「講義・講演音声におけるフィラーの種類と出現傾向について」『話し言葉の科学と工学ワークショップ講演予稿集』69–76.

渡辺美知子(2001)「談話セグメント境界におけるフィラー・連結詞の音響的特徴について」『日本音響学会2001年秋季研究発表会講演論文集Ⅰ』277–278.

渡辺美知子(2001)「講義の談話セグメント境界におけるフィラーの出現傾向について」『第15回日本音声学会全国大会予稿集』85–90.

渡辺美知子(2002)「模擬講演におけるフィラー使用頻度パタンの分類」『第16回日本音声学会全国大会予稿集』145–150.

渡辺美知子・伝康晴・広瀬啓吉・峯松信明(2004)「後続句の複雑さに関する聞き手の予測にフィラーが及ぼす影響」『日本音響学会2004年秋季研究発表会講演論文集』第Ⅰ分冊463–464.

渡辺美知子，伝康晴，広瀬啓吉，峯松信明(2004)「節境界の種類とフィラーの出現頻度」『第18回日本音声学会全国大会予稿集』65–70.

渡辺美知子，伝康晴，広瀬啓吉，峯松信明(2005)「節境界のポーズ・フィラーが非母語話者の聞き取りに及ぼす影響」『日本音響学会2005年春季研究発表会講演論文集』第Ⅰ分冊325–326.

渡辺美知子，伝康晴，広瀬啓吉，峯松信明(2005)「フィラーの出現確率予測における節の種類と後続節長」『日本音響学会2005年秋季研究発表会講演論文集』319–320.

渡辺美知子，広瀬啓吉，伝康晴，峯松信明(2005)「句境界のフィラーが聞き手の予測に及

ぼす影響」『第19回日本音声学会全国大会予稿集』37–42.
渡辺美知子, 広瀬啓吉, 伝康晴, 峯松信明(2006)「音声聴取時のフィラーの働き―「エート」による後続句の複雑さ予測―」『日本音響学会誌』62(5), 370–378.
渡辺美知子, 広瀬啓吉, 伝康晴, 稲垣 貴彦, 峯松信明(2007)「フィラー使用頻度パターンによる学会講演の分類」『日本音響学会2007年春季研究発表会講演論文集』303–304.

# Index

## a

absolute boundary   68, 69
academic ones   42
academic presentations   35, 36, 38, 39, 40, 41, 44, 45, 47, 48, 50, 52, 55, 56, 58, 59, 60, 61, 62, 63, 71, 80, 81, 123
adverbial clauses   66
age   34, 35, 36, 39, 40, 41, 42, 43, 44, 45, 46, 47, 48, 61, 62, 126
*ano*   11, 14, 15, 34, 38, 41, 47, 49, 50, 51, 52, 53, 54, 58, 60, 61, 62, 63, 101, 105, 121, 122, 124
articulation   17

## b

basic clause   17, 19
boundary hypothesis   21, 65, 66, 71, 72, 79, 81, 86, 123, 124
boundary strengths   73, 77, 83, 84, 85, 86, 87, 124, 126
boundary type   71, 76, 77, 78, 79, 81, 83, 84, 85, 87
bunsetu phrase   104, 105
bunsetu phrase boundaries   94

## c

casual presentations   36, 38, 39, 40, 42, 44, 45, 47, 51, 53, 54, 55, 57, 58, 59, 60, 61, 62, 63, 64, 71, 81, 82, 124
Chinese listeners   125
Chinese speakers   119, 126
clause boundaries   14, 20, 21, 22, 27, 67, 71, 72, 73, 74, 75, 78, 79, 80, 81, 86, 87
clause boundary strengths   74
clauses   87
clause type   67, 68, 70, 77
cluster analyses   35, 38, 55
clustering   62, 123
cluster   55, 56, 57, 58
complexity   99, 126
complexity hypothesis   21, 22, 65, 86, 123, 124
conceptual   20
conceptualisation   17, 19, 94
conceptualising   14, 16
conceptual planning   17, 19, 21, 65, 124, 126
conjugation   69, 70
conjunction   73, 74, 75, 83, 84, 85
connective   66, 70
connective particles   66, 69
Core   68, 78, 87
corpus   11, 35, 36
correspondence analyses   38, 48, 55
CSJ   68, 69, 78, 87

## d

deletions   7, 8, 9, 10, 11, 20, 34
discourse-given   25, 26
discourse-new   25, 26
discourse boundaries   20, 21, 83
discourse segment boundaries   78
disfluencies   1, 2, 5, 6, 7, 16, 20, 23, 24, 25, 28, 29, 30, 33, 64, 100, 127
disfluency   10, 21, 61
disfluency types   33,

64, 124, 127
distributional features 126
distributional tendencies 113

### e

*e*   11, 14, 15, 34, 38, 39, 40, 47, 49, 50, 51, 53, 55, 58, 61, 62, 63, 64, 105, 121, 124
*eeto*   11
*eto*   14, 15, 34, 37, 38, 45, 47, 48, 49, 50, 51, 54, 60, 61, 62, 63, 104, 105, 106, 121
expert   114, 117, 119

### f

false starts   24
female speakers   34, 41, 42, 44, 46, 47, 48, 58, 61, 62, 63, 64, 124
fillers   6
formality   63
formal speech   34

### g

gender   34, 35, 36, 39, 40, 41, 42, 43, 44, 45, 46, 47, 61, 62, 126
glottal stops   64
grammatical encoding 18, 19

### h

hesitations   29

### i

idea unit   16, 17
insertions   7, 8, 9
intermediate   114, 116, 119, 120
*Inter Pausal Unit* (IPU) 22

### l

language production   2
language proficiency 100, 125
linguistic encoding   14, 17, 19
linguistic planning   20
listeners' expectations 112, 113
listeners' prediction 125, 126

### m

*ma*   11, 14, 15, 34, 38, 42, 47, 49, 50, 51, 52, 53, 55, 58, 61, 62, 63, 105, 124
main boundaries   78, 79, 80
main discourse boundaries 82, 86
main discourse segment

boundaries   81
male speakers   34, 40, 42, 43, 44, 46, 47, 58, 61, 62, 63, 64, 124
message encoding   19

### n

native listeners   23, 28, 30, 102
non-native listeners 23, 28, 29, 30, 113, 122, 125, 126
novice   114, 116, 119

### o

on-line speech processing 27
on-line speech production 16

### p

pause durations   77
pauses   24
phonological encoding 20
phrase boundaries   86
planning difficulties 19, 23, 86, 112, 113, 120
prediction   28, 99
presentation type   39, 40, 41, 42, 43, 44, 45, 46, 63, 71, 81
probabilistic cues   100
production difficulty

25, 26
production units   19
proficiency   121
prolongations   7, 8, 9, 35, 38, 39, 46, 47, 49, 50, 55, 61, 62, 64, 121, 123, 124

### r

repetition   7, 8, 9, 10, 11, 19, 20, 21, 24, 30, 34, 121

### s

sentence boundaries   20, 21, 22, 67, 71, 72, 73, 74, 83, 85
silent pause durations   78
silent pauses   9, 12, 24, 25, 29, 73, 75, 76, 77, 86, 104, 112
sociolinguistic factors   15, 64, 123, 126, 127
*sono*   11, 14, 34, 38, 46, 47, 49, 50, 51, 53, 58, 61, 122, 124
SOV language   66
speaker attributes   64, 123, 124

speaker variation   3, 33, 34, 123
speaking styles   33
speech level   33, 35, 47, 61, 64, 123, 124, 126
speech planning   65
speech production   5, 16, 17, 22, 30
speech production units   16, 66
speech variation   5
spontaneous speech   1, 2, 16, 19, 35, 66, 73, 99, 125
strong boundary   68, 69
sub boundaries   78, 79, 80, 81, 82
substitutions   7, 8, 9, 10
surface clauses   17
symmetric map   48, 50, 51, 52, 53, 54
syntactic boundaries   14, 20
syntactic complexity   19

### t

*The Corpus of Spontaneous*

*Japanese* (CSJ)   2, 7, 10, 11, 35, 123
Tokyo Japanese   68, 82
*Type A*   68, 69, 70
*Type A* clauses   66
*Type B*   68, 69, 71, 74, 75, 76, 77, 82, 83, 84
*Type B* clauses   67
*Type C*   68, 69, 71, 73, 74, 75, 76, 77, 79, 80, 81, 82, 83, 84, 85, 86
*Type C* clauses   67
*Type D*   68, 71, 73, 74, 75, 76, 77, 79, 80, 81, 82, 83, 84, 86
*Type E*   83, 84, 85, 86

### u

*uh*   13, 24, 25, 26, 29, 121
*um*   13, 25, 26, 30, 121

### v

vowel type fillers   43, 44, 47, 49, 55, 60, 61, 62, 63, 64, 124

### w

weak boundary   68, 69

【著者紹介】

渡辺 美知子(わたなべ みちこ)

福岡県出身。一橋大学社会学部卒業。東京外国語大学大学院地域文化研究科博士前期課程修了。修士(言語学)。東京大学大学院総合文化研究科博士課程単位取得退学。東京大学大学院新領域創成科学研究科博士課程修了。博士(科学)。ドイツ、ミュンヘン大学日本研究センター講師、東京大学教養学部、同留学生センター非常勤講師等を経て、現在、東京大学大学院新領域創成科学研究科助教、国立国語研究所非常勤研究員。日本語の話し言葉の特徴、特に、フィラーを初めとする言い淀みの研究に従事。

〈主な論文〉 Filled pauses as cues to the complexity of upcoming phrases for native and non-native listeners.(*Speech Communication* 50, 81-94. 共著, 2008),「音声聴取時のフィラーの働き —「エート」による後続句の複雑さ予測 —」(『日本音響学会誌』62 (5), 370-378. 共著, 2006),「留学生の日本語力と内容についての予備知識が講義の理解に及ぼす影響力」(『留学生教育』4, 49-65. 留学生教育学会, 1999)

Hituzi Linguistics in English No. 14

## Features and Roles of Filled Pauses in Speech Communication
### A corpus-based study of spontaneous speech

| | |
|---|---|
| 発行 | 2009 年 2 月 14 日　初版 1 刷 |
| 定価 | 11000 円＋税 |
| 著者 | ©渡辺美知子 |
| 発行者 | 松本　功 |
| 装丁 | 向井裕一（glyph） |
| 印刷所 | 互恵印刷株式会社 |
| 製本所 | 田中製本印刷株式会社 |
| 発行所 | 株式会社 ひつじ書房 |

〒112-0011 東京都文京区千石 2-1-2 大和ビル 2F
Tel.03-5319-4916 Fax.03-5319-4917
郵便振替 00120-8-142852
toiawase@hituzi.co.jp　http://www.hituzi.co.jp/

ISBN978-4-89476-407-1　C3080

造本には充分注意しておりますが、落丁・乱丁などがございましたら、小社かお買上げ書店にておとりかえいたします。ご意見、ご感想など、小社までお寄せ下されば幸いです。